# Selected Writings

*Diary Entries and Private Revelations*

CORA EVANS

# Selected Writings

*Diary Entries and Private Revelations*

The Mystical
Humanity
of Christ
*Publishing*

San Mateo
2016

2012 First Printing
2016 First Printing This Edition

**Selected Writings**
Cora Evans
© 2016 The Mystical Humanity of Christ, Inc.

Publisher's Note: All footnotes were added by the publisher and were not included in the original writings of Cora Evans or Father Frank Parrish, S.J.

NIHIL OBSTAT
Rev. Gerald D. Coleman, P.S.S., Ph.D.
July 28, 2015

IMPRIMATUR
+ Most Reverend Richard J. Garcia, D.D.
Bishop of the Diocese of Monterey, California
September 14, 2015

Visit our Websites at CoraEvans.com and ParishRetreat.org

Cover design by Claudine Mansour Design, Mission Viejo, California
Interior design by Sherry Russell Design, Pasadena, California

Library of Congress Cataloging-in-Publication Data
Evans, Cora

ISBN Quality Paperback 978-0-9910506-3-5
ISBN eBook 978-0-9910506-4-2

Printed in the United States of America

PUBLISHER'S STATEMENT

*Selected Writings* is based on the private revelations of Cora Evans.

*Public Revelation—Sacred Scripture*
The Catholic Church recognizes the clear distinction between public and private revelation. Public revelation, meaning the Old and New Testaments, ended with the death of the last apostle. It is complete; the age of public revelation is closed and there will be no new public revelation.

It is no longer public revelation (Sacred Scripture) that grows, but we grow in our comprehension of it.

*Private Revelation—A Possible Means To Growth And Understanding*
The purpose of private revelation is to help a particular soul grow in faith and to develop a greater love of God.

For even though public revelation is already complete, it has not been made completely explicit; it remains for Christian faithful gradually to grasp its full significance over the course of centuries. Throughout the ages, there have been so-called private revelations, some of which have been recognized by the authority of the Church (Saint Bernadette of Lourdes, Saint Catherine of Siena, Saint Margaret Mary, Saint Faustina). It is not the role of private revelation to improve or complete Christ's definitive Revelation, but to help live more fully by it in a certain period of history.[1]

---

1   *Catechism of the Catholic Church* (65,66): Second Edition, revised in accordance with the official Latin text promulgated by Pope John Paul II in 1997.

RECOGNITION

*The Mystical Humanity of Christ, Inc.,*
*Gratefully acknowledges the Extraordinary Generosity*
*of the*
*Theresa and Edward O'Toole Foundation*
*Bert Degheri, Co-Trustee*


PUBLISHER'S ACKNOWLEDGEMENTS

We express special appreciation to Most Reverend Richard J. Garcia, D.D., Bishop of Monterey, California for opening the canonical inquiry into the life and heroic virtues of Cora Louise Evans and thereby declaring her Servant of God. We wish to thank the family members of Cora Evans: Dorothy Evans, daughter and Bob Spaulding, nephew. Also, Irene and Mark Montgomery, June Haver MacMurray (deceased), Al Marsella, CPA and the trustees of the June and Fred MacMurray Foundation, Peter Marlow Jr., Don Ryan, Gabrielle Lien, and her late husband, Warren. Special appreciation is expressed to the Jesuits of the California province, Rev. Michael Weiler, S.J., Provincial; as well as Rev. Vito Perrone, COSJ, and Rev. Gary Thomas for their spiritual support and advice; Michael Huston, advisor, retreat leader and board member; and Pamela McDevitt for her encouragement and guidance.


DEDICATION

The publisher appreciates the role of Fr. Frank Parrish, S.J. (deceased), who entrusted us with the writings of Cora Evans and the responsibility to promulgate the Mystical Humanity of Christ.

# FOREWORD

*Position Taken by Cora's Spiritual Director*[2]

It is important to understand the context in which Cora Evans wrote her various books, short writings and reflections. She was not an author by trade. Cora was given the mission to write. The *rhythm of her daily life* was focused on capturing in written form her ecstasies, visions, raptures, and revelations. It is essential for the Catholic reader to understand the position taken by her spiritual director. His statements reflect the teachings of the Catholic Church. In his composition about the mystical life of Cora Evans, Father Frank includes these observations:

> A writing containing visions and revelations and extraordinary phenomena will usually cause alarm in some quarters. Indeed, the large number of self-styled mystics, of false visionaries and frauds, well justifies great caution and prudent reserve in every case of this sort. On the other hand, it would be absurd to condemn all extraordinary manifestations, as if charismatic graces were no longer to be found in the Church, and all manifestations of the Spirit were to be limited to the early centuries of Christianity.
>
> When confronted with extraordinary phenomena one must proceed by eliminating all possible natural explanations, fraud, illusion, diabolical deception. The virtue of the subject, the spiritual good whereof her mysticism has been instrumental—all have to be taken into consideration. In this case all seems to militate in favor of a true and genuine mysticism. Neither her own imagination, nor her subconscious mind, nor the devil could have caused those visions and revelations that helped her soul to purity of conscience, love of God and neighbor, heroic love of the sufferings of her divine Master, and her ardent devotion toward the Holy Eucharist. It is impossible to explain naturally the hidden depth of spiritual knowledge that has come to her through rapture and ecstasy. Her natural education was little more than grade school—a year and a half of high school and no more.

---

2  *Father Frank Parrish, S.J.*, an exemplary Jesuit priest: Born August 9, 1911; entered the Society of Jesus October 6, 1929; ordained June 13, 1942; entered into eternal life December 29, 2003.

Subconscious and imagination cannot be the cause of such supernatural effects, much less could the devil be the promoter of so much spiritual good. In her own personal life, she has reached a very close union with God. There is nothing she fears more than to offend the divine Majesty of her Lord.

Father Frank continues,

It is very easy to convince oneself of the abundance of charismatic graces that adorn the soul of Cora Evans, merely by reading her writings or by listening to her inspired spiritual talks. Keeping in mind that she is a woman with little worldly education, her words of wisdom, her words of knowledge about the most exalted mysteries of religion, are charisms. What is still more extraordinary is the fact that in all her revelations, divine messages, etc., nothing is ever found that is not in accordance with sound theology. Many new details about Catholic truths, deeper knowledge of theological truths, add new light and evidence to the deposit of faith, especially regarding the humanity of Christ, the Holy Eucharist, and the indwelling of Christ. These charisms are not easily recognized by all.

# Contents

# 1

# Introduction

"Be careful when you say yes to a Jesuit," was my opening statement when meeting with Father Michael Weiler S.J. (Father Mike), Jesuit provincial for the California province. It was intended as a lighthearted opening to a story that began twenty years earlier when my uncle, Jesuit *Father Frank Parrish, S.J.* asked me to be custodian for the writings of Cora Evans. As a very young child, I met Cora when she visited our home. Later I was privileged to read a few of her writings in manuscript form. I was well aware of my uncle's role as her spiritual director. Naturally I answered, "Yes" to his request. And after a brief pause I asked the question, "What's a custodian?" In the years that followed, it is our Lord who continues to answer the question.

Cora was a convert from Mormonism, a writer of profound texts, a mystic who had visions of Jesus, and a woman who had the stigmata. "Are you sure you got the right guy?" is my question to Jesus, and my way of fending off personal fears about the magnitude of this effort.

When I reflect on what has transpired since 1992—*over ten thousand people attending our retreats, conducting more than one hundred events (retreats and lectures), bishops'[3] participation in our retreats, receiving inquiries from people all across the country, the acceptance of our petition for the cause of Cora Evans, the cause being opened by the*

---

3   *Cardinal William Levada, Prefect, Congregation for the Doctrine of Faith:* Former Archbishop of San Francisco, selected our organization for Archdiocesan "Year of the Eucharist" retreat; *Archbishop George Niederauer, Archdiocese of San Francisco:* Advisory Board member, participant in numerous retreats, granted Imprimatur for Cora Evans Intercessory prayer; *Archbishop John Wester, Archdiocese of Santa Fe,* selected us to conduct "Year of Saint Paul" for his former diocese of Salt Lake City; *Bishop Gerald Wilkerson, Archdiocese of Los Angeles,* participated in Parish retreat; *Bishop Patrick McGrath, Diocese of San Jose,* participated in Parish retreat; *Bishop Emeritus John Cummins, Diocese of Oakland,* participated in Parish retreat.

*Bishop of Monterey,*[4] *having as our postulator the priest/canon lawyer who served as Promoter of Justice for the Cause of Saint Damian, and meeting with members of the Roman Curia in the Vatican*—I just shake my head and say "Thank you, Jesus."

What's a custodian? Saint Ignatius said it best, "Behave as though everything depended on you, but know that everything depends of God." Having Jesus as a boss means placing the outcome in His hands, making one decision after another while not knowing where it may lead or the way in which life will unfold. It is living in the best of both worlds.

So here we go again, venturing into an area unknown. For years I've wondered about, and prayed about, publishing. An operative question has been timing. It was never a question of *if* we would publish, but *when*. Since the cause for Cora Evans' canonization officially opened,—everything changed. Suddenly there is demand nationwide and in Europe. And so we move forward, beginning with *Selected Writings*.

*My Two Points of View about Cora Evans*
*First*: I enjoy reading about Cora's life and the choices she made. In this view, I see her life unfold as a young girl growing up in cult-like society, a child who struggles in school, and a young married woman who endured the loss of a child. As I scrutinize her life, I take into account a woman who renounced the religion of her family and a person who for ten years struggled to find God.

Her conversion story is fascinating. Having decided against even considering the Catholic faith, an illness prevented her from getting out of bed to change the radio station when Monsignor Duane Hunt, future bishop of the Diocese of Salt Lake City, gave a talk about the Blessed Mother. As soon as she recovered, Cora visited Saint Joseph Parish near her home in Ogden, Utah. A series of meetings followed, and Cora was baptized on March 30, 1935.[5] Her husband and children were baptized a few months later.

My heart goes out to her when I consider how she must have felt to be abandoned by her own family members and personal friends. Cora's husband, Mack, was unable to find steady employment. They lived

---

4   *Most Reverend Richard Garcia J. Garcia, DD,* Bishop of Monterey, California
5   The March 30 date is noteworthy in that she passed away twenty-two years later, March 30, 1957.

14

in an incestuous cultural environment that considered Catholicism intolerable, actively taught explicit falsehoods about the Church, and created a counterfeit Jesus and man-made gods in the process. What I find truly amazing is that not only did Cora demonstrate great courage in converting; she lived her faith by actively evangelizing many other Mormons[6] to follow her lead.

From various letters and documents written about Cora I understand her demeanor and characteristics, and I can relate to her personal interests. I can identify with parents getting their children off to school and making every effort to keep up financially. In this regard, Cora may be seen as a very ordinary person with a typical American family and lifestyle.

*Second*: This point of view of Cora is unique. In this view I probe the depths of my Catholic faith. It is not possible to comprehend fully the meaning of phrases such as, "I was taken into ecstasy" and "I felt my soul drawn away into a spiritual embrace of love." I find her mystical gifts (fragrances, stigmata, bilocation, ecstasy) interesting and worthy of investigation, but it is the message that captivates me. It is easy to become engrossed in a diary entry or spend hours rereading a short story. Father Frank, Cora's spiritual director, used the term "illuminations" to describe the insights offered in her writings. At times I need to push away from the text and allow time to digest it. Always, I am drawn closer to our Lord. There is no other reason to read Cora's writings.

### Mission and Feeling Utterly Helpless to Accomplish It

Our Lord entrusted Cora with the promulgation of the *Mystical Humanity of Christ* as a pattern of life and a way of prayer for the faithful

---

6   Unlike baptism in Christian religions, Mormon baptism is not valid in the Catholic Church. There is a fundamental doctrinal disagreement. The Catholic faith teaches belief in one God. The Mormon belief is that three gods decided to unite and form the divinity in order to bring about human salvation. Mormons believe God the Father is an exalted man, a native from another planet, who has acquired his divine status through death similar to that of human beings, this being a necessary way of becoming divine. God the Father has relatives, which is explained by the Mormon doctrine of infinite regression of the gods who initially were mortal. In Mormon doctrine, God the Father has a wife, and they procreated sons in the spiritual world. Their firstborn, according to Mormon doctrine, was Jesus Christ. Mormon baptism does not in any way contain the doctrinal belief that is associated with the Christian doctrine of the Trinity or Original Sin or that baptism was instituted by Jesus Christ. According to the official teaching authority of the Catholic Church as pronounced in July 2001 by the Congregation for the Doctrine of the Faith people who were baptized in the Mormon religion "must be baptized in the Catholic faith upon their conversion because they were never validly baptized as commanded by Jesus and taught by the Catholic faith."

worldwide. In her diary entry dated January 29, 1947, Cora expresses vulnerability and admits to feeling inadequate, "I felt utterly helpless to face such a mission as spreading the Mystical Humanity of Christ and the hope of overcoming through God's grace the Mormon heresy."[7] Heroic courage is manifested in the choice to continue in spite of feeling helpless.

### Saints Are Known by Their Stories

There is a consistent theme in lives of the saints. Their lives were given freely to the Lord in response to the circumstances at the time and for the good of the whole Church. Many saints did not ask for or expect to be in the situations in which they found themselves. These men and women radiated the holiness of God dwelling within them. It is the story of their lives, how they responded to grace, the intervention of God in their lives, and their impact on others combined with God's proof by miracles in their name that lead the pope to declare we know for certain this person is with God in heaven.

### Only God Can Make a Saint

At this stage there is no certainty that Cora Evans will become a Saint. We always make this point clear when sharing Cora's story and the fact that her cause is underway.[8] The investigative process for canonization is a search for the truth. It is thorough, time consuming, costly. Only God can make a Saint. For now, we are doing our part by sharing Cora's writings, giving lectures, and conducting retreats.

Readers can draw their own conclusions about the messenger and the message. Following are some reflective questions to assist them:

*In what way did Cora Evans respond to the choices given to her?*

*Did she faithfully follow Christ? How would Jesus prove her loyalty to Him?*

---

7   Heresy is from the Greek word *haireo*, "I take away." The term can be used to mean taking away selected doctrines from Christianity. It is a way of blurring the distinction between religions. The same words are used, but they convey vastly different meanings. In this context, heresy is especially damaging in that it misleads people by teaching false doctrines, practices, and a fabricated version of Jesus.

8   Congregation for the Causes of Saints, *Sanctorum Mater, Instruction for Conducting Diocesan Inquiries in the Causes of Saints*, May 17, 2007, Article 88.

*Is there evidence that she arrived at that perfect union with Christ, which is holiness?*

*Did she endure suffering for her faith? In what way did she demonstrate her fidelity to the Catholic Church?*

*Is Cora Evans a model for the faithful (as wife, mother, convert, contemplative) in keeping with her state in life?*

*In what way did Cora Evans fulfill the mission entrusted to her?*

*What were the circumstances regarding obtaining a spiritual director, and did she follow his guidance in all matters of faith and morals?*

*In what way does the Mystical Humanity of Christ have its roots in Sacred Scripture and tradition?*

*Does the promulgation of the Mystical Humanity of Christ benefit the whole Church?*

*In what way does this way of prayer draw people to the Eucharist?*

Research, written testimonies, and eyewitness interviews, combined with the story and purpose of Cora Evans' life as ascertained from her diary and writings, answered our questions and uncertainties. As we examined her life, we concluded that Cora Evans gave us an outstanding testimony by the heroic practice of virtues and a way of prayer that draws people into a closer more intimate relationship with Jesus. It is our hope that her writings will ignite and renew the faith throughout the United States and eventually the world.

Like all devotions, movements, and reforms in the Catholic Church, the Mystical Humanity of Christ is rooted in Scripture.[9] It is both a way of prayer and a pattern of life: living each day with a heightened awareness of the living indwelling presence of Jesus. It is Eucharistic

---

9   Jn 14:17, 23; Jn 15:4–8; Jn 17:10–11, 22–23; Rom 8:8–11; 1 Cor 1:29–30; 1 Cor 3:16; Eph 3:14–19; 1 John 4:12–13.

spirituality, so important for the growth of the Church in our country. *Pope Benedict XVI* reinforced its significance, "Every great reform has in some way been linked to the rediscovery of belief in the Lord's Eucharistic presence among His people."[10] Today, it is spreading its roots in the Western United States and beyond.

*Prayer and Future Vision*

My prayer is that someday a future pope will *declare with certainty that Cora Evans is with God in Heaven* and enter her name in the Canon of Saints. By that time, millions of people will practice the way of prayer referred to as the *Mystical Humanity of Christ* and the number of conversions to the Catholic faith will be immeasurable. The mass conversion will highlight the missionary nature of Cora's calling.

In my vision, renowned theologians will have read Cora's profound writings and gained new insights into the Christian mystery. The writings will be viewed as supportive of the precious deposit of Christian doctrine: Sacred Scripture, the living Tradition in the Church, and the spiritual heritage of the Fathers, doctors, and saints of the Church.

*Recommendation*

Cora had a single recommendation for readers: first make a visit to the Blessed Sacrament. She always placed Jesus first and wanted others to do the same. It is a grace from God that you now have this book and that you will have the opportunity to read many others.

Always go to Jesus first. Perhaps say a prayer for insight; a prayer of gratitude also would be most appropriate.

*Child of Grace* often appears as Jesus' salutation to Cora. It is a greeting He offers you as well.

Blessings,
*Michael McDevitt*
Custodian for the Writings of *Servant of God* Cora Evans

---

10  *Sacramentum Caritatis ( The Sacrament of Charity)*, post-synodal Apostolic Exhortation, February 22, 2007.

## THE CAUSE FOR CORA EVANS

After thorough review of the writings of Cora Evans, the story of her life and the heroic choices she made, the untold personal sacrifices and the suffering she endured for the cause of our Catholic faith, her outstanding evangelical virtues, the testimony of her distinguished spiritual director affirming her mission, the abundance of eyewitness statements, the vast number of accounts written about her, the hundreds of Mormon conversions to Catholicism she personally influenced, the impact she had on the spiritual lives of people, the effect the Mystical Humanity as a way of prayer continues to have on the lives of thousands of the faithful today—and her mystical gifts which serve as an additional sign of authenticity—we are convinced of her creditability and conclude: Cora Evans was commissioned by our Lord to promote the Mystical Humanity of Christ as way of prayer for the faithful throughout the United States and eventually the world.

For these reasons the cause for Cora Evans will benefit the Universal Church.

## HOW TO RIGHTLY UNDERSTAND
## PRIVATE REVELATION

The Second Vatican Council notes three essential ways in which the Spirit guides in the Church, and therefore three ways in which the world grows: through the meditation and study of the faithful, through the deep understanding which comes from spiritual experience, and through the preaching of "those who, in the succession of the episcopate, have received the sure charism of truth" *(Dei Verbum, 8)*. In this context, it now becomes possible to understand rightly the concept of private revelation, which refers to all the visions and revelations that have taken place since the completion of the New Testament.

Pope Benedict XVI

# 2

# Catholic Doctrine

*Regarding Theological Studies of Cora's Writings*

Theology is described as "faith seeking understanding" for the benefit of the whole Church. The writings of Cora Evans will result in fruitful study by professional practitioners of Catholic theology in every setting—university, monastery, or seminary; and in virtually every branch of study including: Christology, anthropology, sacramental theology, moral theology, pastoral theology, and Marian theology. Anyone studying reported revelations, the experience of mystics, and the associated phenomena will benefit from her works. In addition, Catholic priests who are directing the soul of a mystic will benefit from notes taken by Cora's director, Father Frank Parrish, S.J.

Cora Evans was not a theologian. Because of illness, she had sporadic attendance in elementary school and less than two years of high school. She learned to type while attending a secretarial training course.

In every circumstance she submitted to the will of her spiritual director. This fact is apparent from her writings and the testimony of Father Frank Parrish, S.J.

A convert to the Catholic faith, she lived in full conformance to the teaching authority of the Catholic Church. The majority of her writing was accomplished many years after her conversion. Cora's spiritual director was present when many of the events described in the excerpts, included herein, were revealed during ecstasies.

*Catholic Doctrine on Divine Revelation*

*Dei Verbum* (Dogmatic Constitution on Divine Revelation) sets forth authentic doctrine on divine revelation and how it is handed on. Regarding revelation itself, the Council Fathers affirmed, "In his goodness and wisdom, God chose to reveal himself and to make known to us the hidden purpose of his will (cf. Eph 1:9) by which through Christ, the Word made flesh, man might in the Holy Spirit have access to the Father and come to share in the divine nature (cf. Eph 2:18; 2 Pt 1:4). Through this revelation, therefore, the invisible God (cf. Col 1:15, 1 Tm 1:17) out of the abundance of his love speaks to men as friends (cf. Ex 33:11, Jn 15:14–15) and lives among them (cf. Bar 3:38), so that he may invite and take them into fellowship with himself" (*Dei Verbum* 2).

We await no further new public revelation:

To see Jesus is to see his Father (Jn 14:9). For this reason Jesus perfected revelation by fulfilling it through his whole work of making himself present and manifesting himself; through his words and deeds, his signs and wonders, but especially through his death and glorious resurrection from the dead and final sending of the Spirit of truth. Moreover, he confirmed with divine testimony what revelation proclaimed, that God is with us to free us from the darkness of sin and death, and to raise us up to life eternal.

The Christian dispensation, therefore, as the new and definitive covenant, will never pass away and we now await no further new public revelation before the glorious manifestation of our Lord Jesus Christ (cf. 1 Tm 6:14 and Ti 2:13). (*Dei Verbum* 4)

In his classic book, *A Still, Small Voice: A Practical Guide on Reported Revelations*,[11] Father Benedict J. Groeschel, C.F.R. reinforces Catholic doctrine, "It is important to keep in mind that private revelations have no significance apart from the public revelation of Sacred Scripture, interpreted by the traditional teaching of the Church." He continues, "Public revelation is available to all. It is most important to keep this truth in mind."

Father Groeschel adds, "Public revelation is given to the people of God in Scripture and is addressed to all for all times. It must be accepted and believed. Public revelation in this precise sense ended with the close of the apostolic age."

---

11  Benedict Groeschel, C.F.R., (1933–2014). *A Still, Small Voice* (San Francisco: Ignatius Press, 1993)

The Catholic Church does not derive its teachings from private revelation.

### God Continues to Reveal Himself
In the words of Father Groeschel, "The end of public revelation does not at all mean that God no longer reveals himself to his children. He continues to do so, but now indirectly in what we call private revelations, as well as by other means of his divine Providence."

### Regarding the Content of Private Revelations
The content of private revelation must be read in the spirit in which it is written and interpreted through the teachings of the Church.

Father Groeschel offers this opinion, "Sometimes, however, revelations are given to individuals to be shared." He cites examples of Saint Hildegard (mystical experiences from early childhood, author of *Scivias* (Know the Ways), Saint Bernadette (message and promises at Lourdes), Saint Joan of Arc (responding to mystical voices, she inspired French army), Saint Catherine of Siena (the mystic who called Pope Gregory XI back to Rome), Saint Margaret Mary Alacoque (to whom Jesus communicated the Sacred Heart devotion).

The most recent addition to our abbreviated list of saint-mystics who were given a message to be shared is Saint Faustina Kowalska (1905–1938, called by Jesus to promote the mystery of the Divine Mercy), who was canonized by Pope John Paul II on April 30, 2000. The Holy Father also proclaimed Divine Mercy Sunday for the Universal Church.

### Mystical Communication
The following excerpt from *A Priest Forever* by Cora Evans provides insights into the mystical language expressed in her writings.

### Assumed and Positive Knowledge (1953)
Quickly my spirit was caught up into divine slumber and I looked with Jesus into the artistry of contemplative delight, where His adornments of grace, symbolized as ornaments—either trinket or thought— lay before us in the archives of the skies' cathedral's endless columns. As Jesus and I walked through the great arch, where all wisdom and

knowledge become as one thought, He spoke, or rather infused into me—for here language is no language—the following expressions.

"This columned arch through which we are walking displays every emblem in life. These three great waving banners at the entrance explain the great mental decisions learned through discipline in the greater forms of prayer. The first one is entitled *conscience*. The other two are the lesser gifts that accompany it, *caution* and *criticism in rightful defense.*

"I will explain these to you later and give you the great gift of understanding which will help you corporally to explain them to the world as My Father wills. I want intellectual light to be thrown on these banners in such a way that they will become a challenging desire for My particular friends in the future, the better for them to learn the dignified mystical language to which all are called.

"The first step in the discipline of the mind, through prayer in the mystical language, is to study the divine symbols which form a language which I impart to spirit, in the body, without the use of words. I do not speak an earthly language nor am I ever heard with vocal [sound] by anyone. The grace to use the assumed words 'He spoke' I give to souls who have undergone the ordeals of ecstasy and rapture. They understand My spiritual tonalities which later they form into earthly words in accordance with their own expressions of thought fitting to their refinement and nationality.

"I will give you an example. Meditate upon the thought that you are a perfectly tuned and most priceless violin. Remember, it cannot lose its perfect tuning, the symbol of sanctifying grace, as long as it is properly handled, shielded, or held carefully. Would you loan an instrument like this to a child in a muddy street and allow him to play with it with careless playmates who do not know its value, nor its long years of seasoning and mellowing which caused it to become rich in great depths of tone? Like a soul's tireless years of discipline and austerities? Your answer would be 'no.' That is how highly I regard souls who are habitual dwellers in the higher states of sanctifying grace. They are beautifully tuned to Me. Through the years I have slowly tightened the tuning pegs, hoping the case (spirit) would mellow to such fineness that it would never warp nor crack under the strain of a great chord as it is played for My Father.

"Those slow mellowing tones, or colloquies, are Heaven's earth-sped music, through which Heaven's citizens find joy and pleasure. Into the gifted souls from whom the music comes I form a continuous reciprocation of intellectual thoughts, or the actual gifts of rapture and ecstasy, which I prefer to have known as divine slumber.

"While a gifted friend is in divine slumber, the real artist is the one who lifts the bow and strikes the strings into a chord of Heaven's reverberations which will never be forgotten to the world. That artist is the priest or the spiritual director who governs the music. He becomes even a greater artist by giving, without hesitation, the meditations or lessons of meditations to that gifted soul for his weekly practice. When a friend is graced with rapture, or divine slumber, his state is of the higher perfection in meditation, and his prayer-music for My Father's delight is far more sublime than any other, except, of course, the sacrifice of the Mass.

"It is important to remember that I give immediate grace to transcribe into discernible words the infinite spiritual delights received by the spirit in those higher flights of prayer. This is usually a slowly acquired gift, accomplished by means of careful study, which in turn advances the flights. That study, through calm meditation, is rewarded by wisdom and the other gifts of the Holy Spirit. He teaches all things. But He is a strict disciplinarian and desires clear, calm thinking and deliberate, slow study of simple prayer,—meditation, and contemplation.

"Now, that priceless violin, or soul, is Mine because it is in sanctifying grace. I appreciate value and will not allow it out of My care until death removes the earthly dangers of excessive freedom, unless the soul itself wills otherwise. If a friend gives himself completely to Me, he is Mine, and I'll do with him what I will. I may take the symbol-violin on the stage of time, or I may play it once in life and then close the case and lay it away for the greater gifts of eternity. I have many such instruments—or I might call them jewels—on earth, too priceless for public view.

"I want further to use the symbol idea of the violin as a lesson to give friends certain delights and gifts of knowledge. Suppose I place the violin on a table. Suddenly, a door slams, making a great noise. Instantly the violin is jarred, and without human touch, the strings vibrate. The sound of a beautiful chord is heard, the violin's own tones. No one touched it, but My power did, for I created sound waves. Think of that vibration, or reverberation, as being the same as when I take a friend to Me in the delights of rapture, or divine slumber. My embrace or nearness during divine slumber causes My friend to become the possessor of infinite knowledge. If you heard the chord of the slamming door a hundred times and then suddenly did not know a door slammed, and yet heard the violin, you could truthfully *assume* a door did slam. You could say, 'A door slammed.' That is how certain friends are attuned to Me.

"However, the expression is only a partial truth, or an *assumed thought,* because you did not with knowledge *see* or *hear* a door close or hear it click against the lock. You could not *truthfully* say whether it was a screen door or a solid oak door that closed, supposing their noise to be the same. Yet, the effects on persons in a room would be greatly influenced by the type of door and whether or not it really closed, or merely clicked shut, and then opened. Was it open in the first place, or did someone open it?

"There is great danger in assumed truths which are not truths at all, but sometimes permissible. A moment ago I spoke of the spiritual director as the real artist who lifts the bow and who draws the heavenly music from the strings. When he so directs a soul in divine slumber, assumed truths are cast aside and that soul gives only the most minute and exact details of conditions and states, in other words, *positive knowledge.* My friends should always be able to defend and to define the expressions *assumed knowledge* and *positive knowledge.*

"I want you to teach and to write of the grave need and importance of exact discernment. It is absolutely necessary when man is given the knowledge with which to express the depths and the different meanings in Purgatory and Hell.

"I have told you before that you stand alone on the knowledge of this subject because so many writers and souls gifted with mystical phenomena have given *assumed* thoughts rather than exact tonalities in regard to the states and conditions I just mentioned."

Note: The manuscript concludes with this paragraph: "Write all these things I have told you. I want My friends to know what a priest is and to know also the deeper characteristics of divine slumber with their expressions of positive and assumed knowledge."

# 3

# The Diary of Cora Evans: Excerpts

*Introduction*

Cora Evans kept a journal-type diary of mystical experiences from June 1947 until March of 1949. The diary includes notes by Father Frank, examples of mental questions asked by him during ecstasy, his recorded transcription of her statements, and her explanations.

*Excerpts from Diary Entries*

*June 20, 1947*

On this day Father Frank asked me to keep a regular diary of raptures and ecstasies, along with any other phenomena which may arise in my life. Only through the grace of God do I find the courage to write about the blessings in my life. May the following pages to be written be accepted for the glory of God, and as a means of showing my thanksgiving to Father Frank for his great kindness to us. In humility and submission to any will of my own and in the wisdom of Holy Mother the Church, I lay aside all personal thoughts and desires as I write the following pages in the diary of daily happenings either through simple prayer or in ecstasy.

> *"Only through the grace of God do I find
> the courage to write about the blessings in my life."*

*July 10, 1947*

On this day I began to sleep directly on a board for health and penance for my past sins.

*July 18, 1947*
Along with this mystical phenomena, I also felt the sorrow of great loneliness for Jesus Himself. Tears and a broken heart seemed to take possession of my soul, and then in a moment of great rapture I felt Christ's love. I cannot remember anything of a nature which could be put into finite words to express the indwelling of Christ or His embrace of love.

*July 21, 1947*
I had just finished with reading the Little Office when I was suddenly caught up into ecstasy, and there I knelt before our blessed Lord. Tonight He was dressed as Christ the King in flowing white robes. On His fingers reposed several ruby rings, and in His hand He clasped a beautiful crosier. He moved the crosier slightly as if in the form of a cross and blessed Father Frank and whispered to me, "I love Frank and bless him."

*July 29, 1947*
In meditations rest at 2:30 p.m., I seemed to watch a white dove flying toward me, and in its mouth reposed the Little White Host, the Blessed Sacrament. Then, from a greater distance it seemed I watched the little dove deposit the sacred Little Host in my heart as I knelt before a communion rail.

*July 30, 1947*
My soul hidden within the embrace of God where the thought of occupation of self is not known nor observed by the senses, I suddenly felt the infinite devotions of God for His creatures within my soul, and suddenly I felt the sudden pain and saw the terrible Wound in the hand of Jesus (wound in *my* right hand[12] beginning to appear).

*August 1, 1947*
At 8:30 p.m. I felt myself sinking into the sleep of ecstasy. At this moment I spiritually received a blessing sent to me by Father Frank (later, Father Frank said he had sent me a blessing at that hour). Im-

---

12  i.e., the Stigmata

mediately I was drawn into the unutterable radiance of ecstasy, and while being lifted into the embrace of God, I felt an excruciating pain through both wrists. In the attraction of spacious light, I found myself walking beside Jesus on a narrow bridge. The bridge seemed to be a beam of golden light spanning the darkness of the vast heavens above us. Jesus was carrying His violin under His left arm (in months past I have seen Jesus with His violin, and He told me when I heard Him play, it would be then He would take me in real death). When I saw the violin, the memories of the former vision returned, and I wondered whether or not He was going to play the violin. I felt no concern as to whether I should live or die; at this moment I believe I felt in my soul the great gift of holy indifferentism and detachment from my own will. It is a moment to be longed and hoped for again; it is a goal to work for through love and prayer; it is a moment of heaven on earth while one lives.

*"I felt in my soul the great gift of holy indifferentism and detachment to my own will."*

Jesus leaned against the bridge railing and placed the violin beneath His chin and raised the bow as if to play, when I spoke these words, "Jesus my Beloved, if I can glorify Thee by staying on earth I am willing to stay for the love I have for Thee." From somewhere a white dove flew through the air and perched on the violin strings, and as it hurried to fly away, its claw snapped one of the strings. Thus the violin was broken, and Jesus smiled and said, "I guess we will wait awhile." As we began to walk along the bridge Jesus spoke, "Cora, about the writing you are doing for Me: I have given you a great gift of expressing. Why don't you use it to better advantage? The three vigils a day are to prepare you for a great ecstasy which will take you into greater depths of knowledge than you have ever received, and from then on I want you to use the gift of writing which I have given you—I want you to write with perfect freedom. You will both see and talk with John the Baptist; are you afraid?" I could not answer, but my thoughts seemed to echo through my soul these sentiments, "I'm thankful—I'm thankful, and with You I'll have no reason to be afraid."

As Jesus finished speaking, all was silent. It was a silence as if we were on wings of activity without sound and without motion, only following the thought of silent delight—following delight for a moment was my blissful repose in God's way of love to my soul. Then again, into the blackness of my own soul I watched the glistening virtues as if diamond dust, throwing light on the gifts of patience, repose, calmness, quietness, peace, perseverance, humiliations, pain, riches, charm, thoughts, angels, and gratitude. All these virtues were glistening stars in the heavens, and in their rise and fall of light it seemed I understood how to eradicate the noticeable defects in my soul. In understanding I cried aloud, "All this—all these gifts to me are Thy mystical body in graces loaned to us. Truly we are treasure chests of God—make us worthy—make me worthy of such knowledge—Oh Jesus, why are You not loved more and more? Help me to win hearts for Thee."

*August 9, 1947*
My soul, hidden in the embrace of God's love, found myself with Jesus on the great bridge which He had taken me on a few days ago. As we gazed into the great depths, I was permitted to see the depths of golden hues turning into reddish hue; all this was the cause of my mental impatience, which I had experienced that day. I resolved to follow Father Frank more closely even in mental thoughts, and as an act of reparation I asked to suffer for someone in an act of charity to please God.

*August 10, 1947*
During an ecstasy I found the parting with Jesus an impossibility. I pleaded for graces to do His holy will and also asked to die for His glory.
   *Allow me to return to earth to help souls—(just like Saint Thérèse).*

*August 26, 1947*
In the depths of ecstasy . . . Suddenly I was in the presence of Saint Thérèse the Little Flower. I asked her to pray for me . . . She answered in these words, "Be cloistered, Cora, more and more." I asked Saint Thérèse's pardon for my neglect to her. I have seldom asked her to pray for me, but ten years ago I did place my Mother under her protection

in regards to conversion, and this year my mother was baptized, and for this great favor I thanked the Little Flower. I asked the Little Flower[13] to ask Jesus to allow me, if I gained Heaven, to return to earth to help souls as she had done.

*"I asked the Little Flower to ask Jesus to allow me, if I gained Heaven, to return to earth to help souls as she had done."*

*September 25, 1947*
At 9:40, I felt myself taken into God's embrace. I asked Saint Aloysius to ask Father Frank to send me his blessing. Father Frank was attending a meeting at Loyola. Later, Father told me he received the strong fragrance of roses and knew I needed a blessing and he sent me his blessing—at once I knew I received it.

*"The world is my keyboard and from it I must draw a picture, a picture of impressions through which ascends that natural mind into the immensities of heaven and time."*

When I received Father's blessing, I was quickly taken away into the immensities of God's wonderful gifts to souls where interruption in thought is not known and where any thought in regards to natural reason is most painful. And now in a creature's way of adoption—for under obedience I am asked to write—I'll try to strike upon the keyboard of natural time while I am in timeless time in ecstasy. I am praying as well as hoping for His grace to strike upon my soul the right chord of intellectual thought, better for me to adopt and convey the Master's wishes to the way of finite mind. The world is my keyboard, and from it I must draw a picture, a picture of impressions through which ascends that natural mind into the immensities of heaven and time.

13  In reference to a discussion in the late December 1953–January 1954 time frame, Cora's sister, Ruth Spaulding writes: it was at this time that she (Cora) told me (Ruth) that she had been granted her request to spend her heaven on earth and to bring roses (petals Father later defined) as Saint Thérèse did.

Into the radiance of ecstasy I seemed to be walking in my own parish church through the Stations of the Cross. As I neared the sixth Station, there before me fell our divine Master beneath the cross. I knelt
quickly to console Him, but before I could touch Him our Blessed
Mother spoke to me, in her outpouring way of love for creatures, this
unfathomable story of mercy, love, and understanding:

> He grieves because creatures do not understand and practice His
> bond of love in the symbol meaning of Veronica's veil. The veil is
> the symbol of individual souls, souls coming so close to Jesus in
> His Humanity that His image is impressed upon their souls, never
> to be effaced—this way they put on Christ. To put on Christ is to
> become a Veronica's veil to Christ; they are then a priceless living
> relic, as it were, living on earth doing His will in the love of unity
> because souls have the blessed assurance of Christ with them. My
> Son's justice was about to strike upon America on September 18,
> but the merciful love of seven victim souls of love in America low-
> ered His sword-clad hand. He burned the chart of His will and cast
> it into the sea of mystical America. He watches this nation in a most
> severe way for indifferentism and coldness to His love; that is why
> you noticed the severe lines in His headdress. Its heaviness told you
> of the weight of His thoughts in regards to justice over this nation.
> Ingratitude is the chief reason for His sorrow; even His own Am-
> bassadors have forgotten their zeal for souls above the riches and
> cares of the world.

From my hand Jesus seemed to take a golden chalice and from it
He poured a stream of many-colored gems into the turbulent sea of
America. The gems tossed here and there and then sank into the black
depths of the sea. I seemed to follow each gem in a hidden desire that
through this grace souls would be led to conversion in Christ. As I
expressed my silent desire, Jesus wept and slowly said, "Many conversions will come from these graces, but many converts will fall away
because of My misunderstanding sons (priests) who do not care for
the poor in spirit and knowledge." Then in a voice of great sternness
and indignation Jesus seemed to shout these words as the winds of
the mystical sea engulfed us, "Wake them up before I strike America

into humble submission. My own have forgotten Me—they do not follow Me."

Jesus seemed to return the chalice to my heart, and as He did so I heard Him say, "Cora, I marvel at your patience and calmness; never has a convert woman in such fineness of soul received such cruel treatment from My priests. I will fortify you from now on—he who harms you harms Me. The graces you have received through the whip of unkind priests has been very great—permit me to use the merit of those graces for priests of little understanding."

The eyes of my soul followed the eyes of Jesus, and there in the arch of Heaven seemed to be a small room whose arch was filled with golden roses. Quickly I recalled in vision's knowledge that I had seen this room before; however, the golden roses were now greater in number and brighter in color. I hastened to look for the rose with a few petals missing—it was a symbolical story taught me long ago in regards to Father (name withheld from this excerpt to protect identity).[14] There it was, a broken rose marring the perfection of the rose-covered little room.

I wanted to touch the golden roses but they were too far away. I remember asking the Holy Spirit to help me when suddenly I seemed to be lifted to the golden roses. Each petal was of thin gold and very fragile as well as exquisite to the touch of the soul. As I seemed to be enjoying the exquisite beauty as well as realizing all this was made possible through the kind understanding of Father Frank, and I recognized everything was his through Christ. Jesus asked me, "What do you think Father Frank would like?" I answered, "To know and feel Your blessed nearness more and more as I now actually feel these roses of grace."

Jesus smiled and said, "That eloquence of grace is his." Then in a very kind tone of voice Jesus continued, "Cora watch your gifts—handle them carefully." I answered in a tone of great trust, "Father Frank won't let them fall."

Jesus was pleased that I acknowledged my littleness and possessed nothing at all, for all my gifts were Father Frank's gifts made possible through his guidance and care. Nothing was mine, and I was glad.

---

14   The cruel treatment of Cora by her first spiritual director, a priest who would end up leaving the Church altogether, is detailed in the petition submitted to the Catholic Church.

*January 1, 1948*

Into a world where hidden prayer is life, and where the beauty and remembrance of Jesus is unceasing activity, I visualized my soul as a person walking on one of many golden paths of prayer. The paths of prayer were like sunrays of slender thread of golden light, and they seemed to beckon my soul into a delightful rapture, wherein the glory of our Blessed Mother's holy light and understanding greeted me with the knowledge that she was standing near her statue in our patio rose-garden.[15]

She greeted me with a smile as she spoke, "On my feast days, I'll be here." I pleaded, "Tell me, Mother dearest, when thy Son's first Blood was shed, did Simeon call you when the sacrifice was over, or did he await your orders?"

The Blessed Mother answered, "When chimes were rung, and incense rose, it was then the sacrifice was over; it was then Joseph released me from his tender embrace of love." I continued to ask, "Tell me, dearest Mother, what outward sign did Jesus offer to let poor Simeon know that He was the Christ? And if Simeon had known the Infant was the Christ, would he have dared to raise the knife?"

> *"Simeon's hands, clothed in pure linen, lifted the Christ Child from the altar of sacrifice into the arms of Mary— Mary, the Mother of earth and Heaven."*

To this our Blessed Mother answered, "While in the embrace of Joseph's arms, and while I hid in the shrine of his heart, it was there I asked the holy angels to protect the Precious Blood as a gift and everlasting pledge of love to Heaven from my heart. And now the drops of Precious Blood, like gems of grace, sweep over souls like a flood. From Simeon's hand the angels took the golden blade knife and gathered the drops of blood as if they were roses into their arms. To all this Simeon stood aghast. Now, he realized he had participated in the sacrament of Blood with the real and living Christ. To his knees, poor Simeon fell,

---

15   Evans' residence in Burbank, California

and into my heart he wept the new law's newest psalm: 'O Mary, only thou dost know thou art the woman—the woman of pure soul—a soul so pure a sword shall pierce. O God, have mercy! O woman, do you know the meaning of that mystical sword; do you know the meaning of this Holy Infant Jesus; and do you know, you are the Mother of the living God? O God, have mercy! O woman, O Mother of God amongst us, thou art wonderful!'"

From the table of sacrifice Simeon brought a strip of linen, the clothing of his Christ, and to our Holy Mother's feet, Simeon knelt, and bid her wrap his hands with Christ's pure linen. For Simeon's hands were now priceless and untouchable. In sheer reverence they were never to be uncovered, not even for a feast. The untouchable hands of Simeon were true relics of meaning. They were the symbolical meaning of death and life—death to the old law, and life to the new. The winding pure linen around Simeon's hands proved to be the wedding tie between the old and the new. Simeon's hands, clothed in pure linen, lifted the Christ Child from the altar of sacrifice into the arms of Mary—Mary, the Mother of earth and Heaven.

*January 2, 1948–10:30 p.m.*
I was taken into ecstasy. I saw our Blessed Lord again; He was dressed as a Bishop in golden vestments, and He spoke, "It is the end of a happy day, and you are very tired." [I answered,] "Jesus, what should I do when people love me for that which I am not?"

Jesus answered me, "My heart is like a harp; it reverberates with the effects of your love as you have felt the effect of Father Frank's blessing upon your soul."

For a moment I was allowed to hear the music of the Master's heart. Its melodious tones—its tinkling bells, and the music of rushing brooks calmed with the silent hush of weeping clouds—all told a story of divine love in God. I reached my hand forth as though to touch the intricate strings on the Master's harp, and there I seemed to strum a melody, and I sang aloud as the music rolled into mighty depths and heights, "O let me go—let me go—let me follow where these tones doth flow. I would like to die for other souls, better for souls on earth to feel Thy heavens' warmth and golden glow, for only in this nearness to Thee do souls find their way to Thee."

Jesus sighed, and in that sigh I understood the meaning of His words[16] as He spoke, "but could I deny the world the knowledge of Myself through you? I have taught you in constant conversation in the perpetual nearness of Myself. Knowledge [is] not for you alone, but for the world to know My indwelling in My rightful throne in human hearts."

I answered aloud, "Yes, I know, but I long for the quietness of Thy heart and the understanding of self alone with You which the world cannot give." (I was beginning to hear the noise of the real world, and I shuddered in the pain which it caused my soul and body.)

*January 16, 1948*
On this day our Blessed Lord gave me a beautiful blue ring (mystically). The blue gem was made up of thirty-three smaller stones, all combined as one stone in the setting. It seemed as though our Beloved Jesus reached into the depths of His Heart and took from the fires of His love a tiny golden arrow. The arrow-like pin was gently pinned through the blue stones by Jesus Himself. Jesus told me I would recall the depth of this ecstasy at some future date.

*February 8, 1948*
Late Sunday evening I was taken into a beautiful rapture. It seemed I was kneeling beside my own grave near a seashore. I noticed how quickly the devil-weed grew over my grave, and as fast as I would pull the weed out, the faster it would grow in other places. Tired from pulling the weeds, I conceived upon the plan to gather white rocks— which lay along the shore and with them cover the devil-weed; thus my grave would be beautiful and white. I gathered all the smooth white stones I could find and placed them in rows across the grave, but there were not enough stones to cover the devil-weed and it began to grow up over the stones. In great despair of soul I looked up to the heavens as if to pray and there beside me stood Jesus Himself, dressed as Christ the King in beautiful white- and gold-trimmed robes of heavy embroidery.

---

16  In this passage, Cora is given to understand the purpose of her visions, the importance of writing, and the scope *(for the world to know)* of the mission entrusted to her.

As He removed His cope[17] and laid it across His arm, He knelt down beside me, better to help me with my problem of covering the devil-weed. With one sweep of His strong arm Jesus brushed all the white stones away and then covered the devil-weed with His beautiful cope. It covered the complete grave, and here and there Jesus placed a white rock to hold the cope in place. Then Jesus was gone and I peeked beneath the cope to see what had become of the devil-weed. It was withered-looking, and then it was gone.

*March 9, 1948*
In meditation's gift of hidden prayer, I seemed to kneel embracing the cold feet of Christ as He hung in death on the cross. I could hear my soul praying and pleading in these words: O Jesus, dead on the cross—how I wish You could speak. Without Your tender gaze and way of loving conversation, I fear I'll always be concealed in terrible imperfections; for to whom shall I go,—and who would know my interior soul when even I cannot describe its folly, its soul sufferings and sinful earthly imperfections? O Jesus, all seems lost, for You are my intimate real self, You are life in me, I am the least of myself in this clay form—and now You are dead. As I kneel here to touch Thy cold feet—there is nothing for me to say but this, "I am the poor servant who was too late to help You carry the cross." O Jesus, Jesus, let me die for thee—come down from the cross and live in me. I would not dare to ask this of Thee, but I remember You were born in a cold cave for love of us, and in that love for us I believe You would dwell in my cold cave heart when I ask it through the grace of love. O Jesus, bring into this dark cave of mine all Thy angels and saints, better for the world to know You live again on earth, even in a poor cave where there is neither candle-flame nor food unless You light the candle of love and feed me with Thy Sacred Self. O Jesus, I must have Thy holy Presence and guidance, for who am I to dispense of these holy graces which You have entrusted to me? I believe You will come down from the cross and dwell in me, for have You not said that the Kingdom of Your Father is in our hearts? And now that You are dead—where have

17 An ankle-length vestment worn by a bishop or priest at ceremonies other than Mass; it is draped over the shoulders, and fastened with a clasp. The design of a hood, in the shape of a shield, adorns the back.

You gone but to human tabernacles, for You have said You would not leave us. Therefore You do live again through us when we give You our human body. Thus, clothed in us, You are the Mystical Humanity on earth and in the Mystical Humanity, O God, please govern the graces You have given me.

> *"Thus, clothed in us, You are the Mystical Humanity on earth and in the Mystical Humanity, O God, please govern the graces You have given me."*

*March 12, 1948*

In meditation's way of prayer, I thought about the subject which Father Frank had given me to meditate on for the day: what is gratitude? I asked myself: How can I show my gratitude to God for the many gifts He has given me? He has allowed me both Heaven and earth while I live on earth in this valley of tears. How can I be grateful or show gratefulness to God for His compassionate mercy toward me—for He walked in the shadows of death (the way of the cross) to rescue me from a terrible heresy? O God, my soul cried aloud, let me stand on that tiny footstool and peer through these eyes of mine, in willing submission to Thy will in all things, to see Thee everywhere and in everything, and then when I find You hidden in little things let me always sing aloud with joy, "I'm grateful, dear God, for You are God."

This I understood was all ours: pain, woes and sorrows—these were ours to do with as we willed. I felt a soul-deep satisfaction with this thought in the light of the knowledge that we have something of our own . . . I possessed something and that something was pain, sorrow, and bitter denials. Small were my possessions, but they were mine— and I could offer them back to Him in the spirit of gratitude, for it was all I had to offer God. Then I understood, as co-workers with Jesus in the gift of sanctifying grace, we also possessed a type of accidental powers through the gift of transubstantiation, for at will I could offer these gifts back to God with different intentions such as pain for gratitude, sorrow for love, and trials and tribulations for petition and thanksgiving. How good God is; how thankful I am to possess something to offer Him!

As this meditation ended, I was permitted through the grace of God to see both *Saint Francis Xavier* and *Saint Aloysius,* who gave me their blessing.

*Palm Sunday, March 21, 1948–8:25 p.m. (time of ecstasy is from notes taken by* Father Frank)

Jesus, Jesus—what can I say? (The vision of the terrible scene was beginning to leave the gaze of my spiritual eyes.) O Jesus, bless all my friends, no, don't bless me, for the gift of faith to come into Thy Church is all I deserve. I am not worthy of Thy personal blessing (for a moment Jesus in His Humanity as Christ the King—for the vision of the cross was gone—looked sad because I was refusing His blessing). Then I realized in the fullest detail how I was offending Him by desiring my own will above His gifts; desiring to tell Jesus what to do rather than letting Him have His complete way filled me with great sorrow, and I begged His pardon as I knelt before Him. Jesus smiled and I spoke aloud, "Jesus, when Father Frank hears how I have acted and how I was not obedient to the nothingness of self, what will I say to him? I'm so sorry, Jesus, please bless me. Jesus, I'm not afraid. Father is so Christ-like; he has Your great gift of kindness. Thank You, Jesus, for Father Frank." Our Lord personally blessed Father at this moment. Jesus then turned to me and blessed me and said, "Every Thursday until next Lent you will see Me unless Father Frank makes other plans. I am pleased with the Mystical Humanity propagation."

As Jesus spoke, in visions' way I could see the complete nation of United States. It was in darkness, but here and there were little lights like bonfires flickering in the night. I understood they represented souls on earth who were propagating the knowledge of Christ's Humanity within souls—Christ-bearers, human tabernacles, and the indwelling within souls as understood in the language of Saint Paul: "It is no longer I but Christ in me."

*June 17, 1948*

Instantly, I saw Jesus. He was clothed in emerald green, and His hands were covered with diamonds. I asked Him to bless Father Frank (in San Francisco, giving a group of sisters a retreat). Our Lord said as He pointed to His Sacred Heart, "He is with Me." Again I thanked Him for calling Dorothy[18] to a religious vocation. Then Jesus turned to bless me, and when He blessed He said, "Winging Its way from the Heavens is the Dove of all peace; it is yours, little soul, for willingly accepting My call for Dorothy. In this peace of soul, I'll accept many hours of your life in reparation for parents who rebel at My call when I call either son or daughter to follow Me."

*June 26, 1948*
We attended Mass with Father Frank in the chapel of the Blessed Virgin Mary nuns' convent in North Hollywood. As Father turned from the tabernacle to bless us, there on either side of him stood two beautiful blue angels. Their combined light of blue tints scattered over Father, thus bringing about the effect that Father was sheltered in a nook of blue light.

Later, while [I was] speaking to the nuns, the room slowly filled with the fragrance of incense and roses. The rose fragrance was still lingering on a crucifix that had been blessed ten days before.

*July 19, 1948*
Six years ago I was asked by many friends why I did not have a spiritual director. They feared for my soul in its climb to God alone and also warned me about losing out on special graces, which would and could be mine if I chose to have a director. At this time I did not know the real meaning of a director, nor did I realize that anyone needed one. Sometime later I decided to ask our Jesus, God willing, whether or not it was His will that I ask a priest to direct my soul. When my soul was next carried away in ecstasy I remember asking Jesus the above question and His answer[19] was, "I am preparing one for you."

*August 18, 1948*
I had been very ill for about six weeks, and this day I thought I would die from a weak heart condition as well as the pain from my spine. I

---

18  Cora's youngest daughter, Dorothy Ruth Evans
19  From this diary entry we count back six years to 1942, the time when Jesus made the statement, "I am preparing one for you," and we see the connection: Frank Parrish, who entered the Jesuits in 1929, was ordained a Catholic priest at Cathedral of Saint Mary of the Immaculate Conception (Old Saint Mary's), San Francisco, California, June 13, 1942. Our Lord was preparing Father Frank for his role with Cora for years before he was assigned to his role in guiding her soul.

could not find the desire to live, no matter how I reasoned with myself; all I could think of was the terrible longing to be with Jesus. The inhaling of oxygen did not relieve my heart pain, and so I had put the oxygen mask aside—just waiting for death.

Father Frank called on us, and in his usual kind way he tried to make me reason with myself in the thought there was much to live for, and that I must try to look at the spiritual side of my life in accepting that which was most difficult to accept in life for the glory of God. Father Frank said to me, "Sometimes it is harder to live than to die." These words seemed to penetrate my soul—to awaken a dying soul, and while Father continued to speak I was suddenly caught up into a beautiful rapture.

*September 8, 1948*
. . . We are caretakers of our living tabernacles. We either open or close the doors of self when we are hidden in the vale of tears, which is like a curtain over the tabernacle door. When we brush aside the curtain of darkness, better to be alone with God in our tabernacle of self, we must first forgive all souls who have harmed us in soul and body, for they are tabernacles too. Some tabernacles are soiled; others are dusty, while others are covered with mold, but He does not ask us to enter there—all He asks is for us to keep one tabernacle clean and free for Him, he will take care of the rest. Thank You, Jesus.

Even though I wander into the shadows of death, Thou wilt be my everlasting Host, all the eternal shall seek Thee most, for art Thou not the sacred host? Oh love eternal, Oh love sublime—bless the interior symbolic heart of mine. Dress it in gold, gems, and myrrh, that from its essence of my love in Thee I may understand that—living or dead—I am an eternal tabernacle in Thy eternal caress.

*September 16, 1948*
I asked Our Lord about Father Pio,[20] was he brokenhearted about the false news about him? Jesus bowed His head in sorrow, and I was pierced with a dreadful pain in my heart (mystical pain in His Heart).

20  *Saint Pio (Pius) of Pietrelciana, O.F.M. Cap* (1887–1968), Capuchin Catholic priest, known as *Padre Pio* and recognized for his bearing the stigmata. Canonized June 16, 2002.

I offered the pain in reparation for the many wrongs and misstatements against Father Pio. Jesus asked me to come closer to His Heart in the virtue of trust. To this I answered, "I would try."

> *"I offered the pain in reparation for the many wrongs and misstatements against Father Pio."*

*September 23, 1948*
As I stood gazing upon the shaft of light, its immensities overwhelmed and frightened me. There in its path of gentleness I felt the pain of quiet recollection of that which was sin within me being quenched in the delight of this light of unspeakable wonder. The eyes of my soul could not find the end of the shaft and I wondered, where did it begin and what was it purpose? I could not see through it nor did I care to venture too near it; I was delightfully pleased just to gaze in wonder and astonishment upon its beauty. Where was fear in my soul—I felt none; neither did I feel hindrance, torment, or disturbance. All was a communication of sense in gladness, brightness, and interior peace which could melt away, [yet] somehow I perceived it was something everlasting. Suddenly my soul understood the great beam of silken light was a visible manifestation of the grace of mercy. The shaft of light at its end was heart-shaped. The point removed caused the outline of its shape to resemble the letter M, then I understood, through the grace of God, this was a visible something which really had no form, but in order to manifest a state of nothing to my soul I was given the grace to see the gift of mercy in this light and form . . . while in speechless wonderment I gazed upon the gift of mercy.

> *"Suddenly my soul understood the great beam of silken light was a visible manifestation of the grace of mercy."*

*Ecstasy continued:* As she (Blessed Mother) spoke these words, I was taken in bilocation to a room where knelt our Holy Father.[21] Somehow

---

21  Pope Pius XII, who served as pope from March 2, 1939 until his death in 1958. The cause for his canonization is under way.

I knew he was in the midst of great prayer in reparation for the sins of the world. He was on his knees and bent over on his elbows; in this position he continually kissed the floor with this prayer before each kiss of humility, "Mercy, Our Lady of Mercy, have mercy on my children." After I had watched at least a hundred repeated kisses and listened to the same ejaculation, I noticed our Holy Father was greatly fatigued, and my pity went out to him—wishing I could do something for him. Suddenly, there before our Holy Father stood Jesus Himself, dressed in the majesty of a bishop. His look was stern as though searching over the earth with a gaze of terrible indignation. Jesus put His right foot forward—[invisible to the gaze of our Holy Father, who] repeatedly kissed the Savior's foot. For a moment I sensed that Holy Father knew in a moment's rapture of his soul that Jesus was there before him.

*September 30, 1948*
Today is the birthday of the Little Flower into Heaven, and Saint Aloysius had assured me I would see her sometime this week. I have seen the Little Flower about ten times in the past six years. When I was before the Little Flower, I asked her to teach me how to pray these simple words as she would say them in all the beautiful meaning of love, "I love you, Jesus."

*October 7, 1948*
Father Frank's notes: 8:30 p.m. Cora slowly going into ecstasy—rigidity setting in.

Cora's explanation regarding statements made during ecstasy: While Saint Aloysius asked my petition to have interior suffering rather than visible, which is usually the case when I see Jesus suffering, and I knew I would see Him suffering this day on the cross. While Saint Aloysius appeared in silent prayer, I kept praying aloud, "I have so failed—I have so failed."

Saint Aloysius was telling me the ecstasy and interior suffering would be in union with the Holy Father and his petitions for America.

I asked Jesus whether or not other souls were in ecstasy of reparation at this moment. He (Jesus) answered, "Yes . . . I need them at this hour. I'm sorry more souls fail to find the way to hidden interior prayer, better for them to offer the merit—as you are doing with

Father Frank in union with the gift of transfiguration—for in and through My priests all things can be accomplished." Jesus was sad and my soul spoke aloud, "I so dread this—may I tell them?" This meant I hated above everything else to see Jesus sad, and I asked permission to tell souls about Jesus being sad because of the lack of victim souls.

> *"I love them in different ways—all for the one purpose—I want love above everything else which My creatures can offer me."*

(Jesus continued) "I love all; there are no boundaries in My heart, for souls the world over are my children. I love them in different ways—all for the one purpose—I want love above everything else which My creatures can offer me. Love, offered to Me, can bring peace to individual souls and nations."

When I asked Jesus, "What is it that we love about Your Name, and what does it do to us? It was then I understood Him to say, "My Name is the crown of glory for souls. My Name is power—I love to hear My creatures using My Name for the good of nations and individual souls." As he spoke these words, I stood near Him and happened to glance toward His ruby-covered crown. As I admired His crown I noticed a gem was missing, and I asked Him whether or not He knew it was missing. Before He could answer, I noticed Our Blessed Mother near His side rapidly threading the gems of His tears on a silver chain. While I marveled at so many tears, which resembled a great waterfall, Jesus showed me a beautiful ring on His forefinger, and there in the ring glistened the missing jewel from His crown. Jesus put the ring on my finger, and our Blessed Mother spoke these words, "This is the fifth ring you have received from my Son; the other four rings you returned to Jesus as merit through detachment for the good of souls. This ring I desire for you to keep: it will be the last one you will receive. You will often see it and be reminded of its meaning in the grace of martyrdom to both body and soul. Bless you with the rosary of tears" (she blessed me with the countless tears of our Lord—somehow they seemed to flow into my heart). "Remember always to place the tears in the chalices of souls who love the Master. Never let the ways of the world cause you to cease with loving my Son—never let us hear Him sigh these words when He longs for you, 'You're always gone when I'm so lonely!'"

*October 14, 1948*
At 5:00 a.m. Friday morning, I was taken into an ecstasy, and there I saw our Jesus. He spoke these words to me, "Cora, I understand the loneliness you may choose to go through as well as I understand the loneliness you have gone through. Always unite your loneliness with mine, better then will I be able to brighten the stars, which rise above this hand of mine, which proves to be the dark cross for so many souls. Now in answer to Saint Aloysius's petition for you, I am going to relieve you of the deeper ecstasies until Lent, unless for some grave reason or for a Feast Day with Father's permission you may slumber in God. This form of rest will give you more time for the writings, which I desire you to do for the love of Me. I desire for you to write the wonderful corrections[22] which Saint Aloysius taught you a few years ago, better for souls to rise with courage into the clouds, for the plan of redemption continuing through souls for souls."

Then Jesus gazed at my hand, and there reposed the huge ruby ring, which He had given me a week before. As Jesus touched the gem in the ring He said, "You are not afraid to climb higher; I'll help you. I needed a strong character like you to help me with the plan of redemption for souls; therefore I chose you to live Mormonism to its heights, better for you to be a living example for many souls. It took great courage to turn your back on popular evil [promoted] through their temple, but through your example hundreds of souls are already saved, and in time the devil's heresy will be completely overthrown because you dared to turn your back on evil. This climb ahead of you, turning your back to the world, will be as great in its reward for yourself and souls. Help Me to redeem many more through a living example who was of My choosing.

In a moment of great love for Jesus, I knelt at His feet and cried on His knee. Crying because of loneliness for Him, I found it so hard to leave His gaze. Without thought of obedience or of His will above mine, like a child I pleaded to remain with Him. Then again

---

22  This is an apparent reference to *Letter Lessons* by *Cora Evans*: a series of 31 letters written to Father Frank, "the mystical steps of knowledge given to Cora by Saint Aloysius." Pre-publication edition available.

He showed me the ring on my finger and from His eyes I seemed to understand His love for me, which comforted me in the thought of leaving Him. The morning dawned with my soul feeling the great loneliness that I had anticipated as I gazed upon the high mountain with Saint Aloysius. For the first time I realized the great meaning of Saint Paul's quotation, "I die daily" and with a great saint I too cry, "I die because I cannot die."

*November 1, 1948*
The devil was angry with me, for I threatened to use the cross which they [the demons] hate and suffer under when we command in the name of Jesus for them to kneel before it (I have done this before and have actually heard them moan and cry for release). As I began to kneel before Father (Frank), the sign of a true living cross, they shouted at me to stop or they would send all the Satanic powers after me. Several demons shouted, "Let's knock her down before she kneels before the symbol of the Jesuit powers; she is in league with them." As Dorothy handed me the cross, the devil knocked it from my hand by sort of kicking the back of my wrist, which hurled the cross from my grasp. The evils threatened to get me for being the cause of removing the palm [readers] superstition.[23] The head angel from Satanic powers said he was not any more afraid of holy water than Lucifer was. They were afraid of the Jesuits and the cross.

*November 10, 1948*
Bilocation of my soul to China to baptize infants [Cora's explanation of this ecstasy is included in her diary]

*November 18, 1948*
Earlier in the day I had received eighteen red roses from Doctor Jack, Mary, and Anna in memory of the day we met three years ago . . .

---

23  The *Catechism of the Catholic Church* states, "All forms of divination are to be rejected: recourse to Satan or demons, conjuring up the dead or other practices falsely supposed to 'unveil' the future. Consulting horoscopes, astrology, palm reading, interpretation of omens and lots, the phenomena of clairvoyance, and recourse to mediums all conceal a desire for power over time, history, and, in the last analysis, other human beings, as well as a wish to conciliate hidden powers. They contradict the honor, respect, and loving fear that we owe to God alone" (CCC 2116).

*November 20, 1948*

... I pleaded with Saint Aloysius to ask the Master to bless a few more roses. To this request, Saint Aloysius asked me to choose five roses from the bouquet and place them in the vase with the four blessed roses and he would intercede for me ... The ecstasy lasted about ten minutes and then I was wide awake. I had asked Jesus to take me in death rather than to allow me to offend anyone in my way of giving the rose petals away or in any other way of venial sin. Jesus smiled, and suddenly I was reliving the scene of the roses being placed in or near the fires of His Sacred Heart as of November 18. Immediately we noticed the mystical fragrance of roses on three roses, which Jesus had just placed in His heart. Saint Aloysius' petition had been answered.

Mack,[24] Dorothy, and I were watching the blessed roses when suddenly they began to turn a blue-purple in color and then browned and crisped on the edges ... Toward morning I had a most terrible thought of pride strike upon my soul about the roses. In an act of contrition I asked to have the roses removed from my life as a penance and mortification to my senses. Immediately Saint Aloysius answered, "I have removed them."

*Father Frank's Notes: The Concentration Camp*

At 1:00 p.m., Father Kilp, S.J. and I visited at Cora's home and took pictures of the roses where we had placed them on the shrine ... At 6:15 p.m. Dick Huston arrived; he was going to take pictures of all the rose petals ... At 7:30 p.m. Cora went into deep ecstasy—made Sign of Cross ... Cora speaks, "The two roses (petals) have been dropped in North Eastern Germany over a concentration camp. Four men watched them fall from the heavens—the falling of petals resembled tiny flames of fire falling on the earth. This act of dropping the rose petals on snow-covered ground revived faith in the lonely followers of Christ in the concentration camp. Within minutes several hundred men were listening to the story and venerating the ground and the actual rose petals and leaves. When the actual rose petals were dropped over the camp, then I understood the deeper meaning of the saints on earth working with those in Heaven—here was the indestructible

24 Cora's husband

bridge, the communion of saints. Through mystical phenomena and Christ's blessing on rose petals, the saints are at liberty to take the petals and scatter them where they choose to further the missionary work of Christ. In this way, Christ chooses the material way to further His work for the good of souls."

*Father Frank's Notes continued*
Cora speaks (while in ecstasy), "Why, oh why—into the blue flame of Thy Sacred Heart while the other night Thy Sacred Heart was aflame with white fire, while tonight it is blue. Oh my Jesus, make them love You more and more—what do they think when they see the petals on the snow? What takes place in their souls? Father, Jesus said, 'The fires of His love show the reciprocal return of His creatures' love—today the world is cruel—today the world is cool to His love. This hour His heart is blue because the returning love from His creatures is at a low ebb, and thus His heart mirrors the eternal fires of God from above as well as the reciprocal blue fires returning from creatures—thus both God's light and the light of souls on earth reflect one to another through the Heart of Jesus.' Oh Jesus, that all hearts may know Thee and Thy love—for in Thy heart all earthly loves are mirrored to God for us. Oh blue of penitential night of the world—O mirrored light of the eternal Father, stay the arm of justice—never did I know the deeper meaning of the Sacred Heart. May the fires of our reflected love to and through Father Frank find their way for us like a bridge of love into that Sacred Heart, where we may brighten the flames of blue into the flames of white as an adornment of majesty to God the Father. We trust our love to Thee through Father Frank, for we know he loves the Sacred Heart of Jesus.[25] Those fires, our petitions, are the symbols of our hearts in those flames of love, which he brings to Thee. Oh fires of the Sacred Heart, let us help to erase the blue and bring to life the seething white of love as a penetrating love from our meek humanity fires from within our souls. Bless all my friends; let me be the servant of Thy love—how can You stand by so patiently when You know that when You look into that mirror of Thine own heart—for it

---

25  Father Frank was the Los Angeles Archdiocesan Director of the League of the Sacred Heart and the Apostleship of Prayer.

is us mirrored there—Thou dost only find coolness, disappointment, and burning fires of blue flames? O Jesus of merciful love, charity, patience, and kindness, make us love Thy heart that takes us into the forest of solitude and prayer, better to gaze into the eternal fires of love—make us worthy, make us on our return to love Thee more and more, better to make all hearts fervent."

*November 29, 1948*
At 12:15 p.m. I was taken up into a state of rapture, and there beside me stood Saint Aloysius. He was asking me to obtain permission from Father Frank for him to use the rose petals from the rose, which he had taken mysteriously from the room on November 20. I seemed to understand that Saint Aloysius and the Little Flower, Saint Theresa, were going to drop the rose petals over a certain place in China where many little infants would benefit from their blessing of invisible grace . . . Saint Aloysius was asking for a priest's permission to perform this act of charity, for with permission the benediction would be greater in their missionary desires and labors . . . I phoned Father Frank for the above permission and he gave it.

*December 9, 1948*
This ecstasy was most difficult because of my soul going through the beginnings of a spiritual night of the soul.

Father's notes: 6:10 p.m. Cora's drops arms (arms up for 45 minutes). Cora continues, "Saint Aloysius, I don't want to leave you, bless all my friends, tell me what to do."

M.W.Q. (*mental, written, question* by Father Frank not visible to Cora)—If God wills, come back to us now: Cora answered, "I know that. It's harder to do than to say. Bless Father Frank, because he doesn't know the pain to leave Him (Jesus). When Father Frank dies, give him Thy crown—better for all priests to follow Thy crown of great gifts when they follow him in Thy path of love. Don't let visits of doubt, despair, and dismay lead the way; rather, let Father Frank kindly sway all hearts until they reach the happy day of God's majesty and God's immensity. Don't leave me, Jesus. Let me remember—let me remember in spiritual life they're always seeing God's gifts He has given to me. Let me adore, worship, and reverence Thy Solemnity, because Thou have touched the world in the hands of Thy priests. Make me courageous—joyous . . . I want to endure all things for Thee. Make me humble. Make my heart tremble when I think of Thee—let me come to Thee before too long. I don't care about a place up above— just so I have Your love. Immensities, gratitude, reverence are nothing, God, just Your love to allow me to be just a speck of dust beneath Thy feet when You walk. Help me in the work You would have me do. Help me to see You in Father Frank; the road won't be hard if from time to time I may see the crown on Father Frank. He is humble, kind, and so much like You, Jesus; he has all your qualities—what more does he need? Let Thy crown be visible on him when I'm down; let the crown be ever in his reach. Don't embrace me, Jesus, embrace Father, for I am not worthy."

# 4

# The Writings of Cora Evans: Excerpts

*Heresy—Rosary of Little Brown Birds*
*(Experience began in 1944, concluded in 1947)*

*1944*

In mental prayer, my body seemed to say aloud to my soul as if it were another person, "Oh, soul, thou are lonesome today, sorrowful and sad, walking alone and waiting for the Master's nearness to come to thee in the lonely desert of thy soul. Oh, soul, take courage and reject the impulse to relive and ponder over the footsteps of time gone by. Time is restless, restless as thy heart is restless in its search for God. The narrow path to God passes through the silent desert of detachment, where loneliness in solitary stillness is the knowledge of one's own nothingness and, in that nothingness of self, God relives His life in souls. The way is narrow and most difficult as well as hazardous. It is a pattern of life to follow. It is His way to travel to perfection and must be traveled with the care and faith a traveler would watch his maps, better to watch the course the Master has chartered for thee."

I fell to my knees and in spirit I felt the burning sands of time beneath me. In the depth of suffering in the world of detachment, I called on my guardian and guide, Saint Aloysius, for guidance and protection. I asked him, "Why do I feel the burning sands of time as I kneel in prayer?"

With a tone of gentleness and love, he answered, "Time does not stand still. Fear alone causes you to feel the sting of earth. Try to rise above the sting of attachment. Then you will better follow the Master's desires for you. The burning in your soul is the effects of repeated disappointments in life haunting you, causing you to offer excuses by the hour, thus doing violence to time and merit. Disappointments burning like stubble in your soul are like pagan fires burning before foreign gods. Cease now to honor useless gods. Rise above them by the hour as lessons for humility. The sting of earth when buried in the cloak of humility is dead. It is noiseless unless you allow fear to awaken it. Come with me into the heights of thine own soul where darker musings fade away."

I followed St. Aloysius as one hastening in flight to leave the burning desert. I tried to walk in his footsteps. In doing so a thought of joyous gladness swept through my soul. Surely this was a game with God's saints, their little way in humble patience to lead us to Jesus.

St. Aloysius spoke, "It is the Master's desire for you to follow me into your mission in life. You have been told your fighting in this life is against principalities and powers—great powers of evils which haunt the earth with repeated heresies."

Before us arose a great valley surrounded by high mountains. No flicker of light sped its way to us from its fabulous depths, nothing but the slushing sound of something which reminded me of breaking surf or waves slapping upon one another in their rise and fall with earth's ocean tides. As the eyes of my soul accustomed themselves to such terrible darkness, there in the center of the great valley, pinnacled into the sky, were the spires of the Mormon temple. The slushing sound in and throughout the valley was the rise and fall of a million black snakes as they slapped and fell over one another. Their angry crawling and hissing at one another told my soul of hatred and their jealous watching to protect the temple heresy from the outside world.

As I walked along the top ridge of the great valley, I knew the snakes had knowledge of my presence. Suddenly and in anger, the million snakes (a million devils in the form of snakes) set their eyes on me. They swarmed toward the ridge where I walked. They hissed their fiery breath at me with threats of bodily harm and soul's destruction if I did not cease praying the rosary for their destruction. For the first time I sensed the power and use of the holy rosary over heresy and, as I walked along the snake-hissing valley, I prayed the rosary as I had never prayed its mysteries before. I prayed for the deliverance of souls held in bondage of heresy, for I had once been its victim.[26]

In the path ahead and walking toward me was a priest. He was dressed in a cassock with a purple stole around his neck. In his left hand he carried a black rosary and in his right hand rested an open book of prayers. We stood together looking over the valley of death and prayed the rosary. With the ending of each mystery, the priest raised his hand in blessing and made the Sign of the Holy Cross over the valley of snakes and spoke Latin phrases, which seemed to cause all the hideous snakes to seek shelter beneath the darkness of one another.

As the rosary prayers continued, the snakes, like tidal waves, swept toward us. They tried to climb the steep embankment near our feet, but the power of the holy priest and his Sign of the Cross caused many snakes to fall back into the valley as though dead. The bodies of the dead snakes seemed to form a stepping ledge for the next oncoming tide of snakes in their attempts to reach us. Tide after tide rose and fell before us. Finally, a few snakes seemed to manage to reach the top of the ledge. One great snake threw his head and body toward my feet from over the ledge. He missed my foot by inches, and as he slid into the depths of death, the priest spoke to me these words, "Ask our holy Mother to send the merits of her tears for us upon this heresy."

> *"I felt utterly helpless to face such a mission as spreading the Mystical Humanity of Christ and the hope of overcoming—through God's grace—the Mormon heresy."*

I heard my soul praying, "Oh, holy Mother, lend us thy tears and, through their merit, aid and help us in this our fight with heresy."

Instantly the heavens rumbled, and great floods of driving rain poured into the great valley, washing the snakes away from their moorings from the mountain ledge. The valley filled with water and then we watched the waters recede, leaving the valley washed clean

---

26 Cora often prayed for Mormons. She loved the Mormons and considered them to be her heritage people. Cora's use of the word "victim" is in reference to the early years of her life when she was raised a Mormon and subjected to and duped by false teachings about Jesus.

with the exception of a few weather-beaten snakes who still clung to the temple doors.

Then I heard Saint Aloysius speak, as he seemed to stand near us for me to follow him. I followed him into a glorious path of golden light where stood our Jesus, smiling upon us in His embrace of love where fear doth not enter in.

*Three years later, January 29, 1947*
I felt within my soul the same terrible fear and broodings of mistrust against myself, the same fear and anxiety which I had felt when I stood near the ledge of a million devils, envisioned in the form of black snakes. In this spiritual night of the soul, I tried to find ways and means of handing the torch of my mission, fighting heresy, to some other soul. I felt utterly helpless to face such a mission[27] as spreading the Mystical Humanity of Christ and the hope of overcoming—through God's grace—the Mormon heresy.

I talked to Father Frank Parrish and told him about my fears and doubts and asked for his advice. He assured me God would help me and asked me to continue in the mission of my life for Jesus with new courage and hope. He also assured me he felt sure this was God's work through me, and when doubts assailed me again, I must try to remember Father Frank as God's ambassador and trust in his judgment for the care of my soul and mission. This I promised to remember.

That same evening, I was assailed with greater doubts and fears, as well as thoughts of pride, in the graces God had given me. I tried to believe and remember the words of hope and trust Father Frank had given me. Desperately I tried to believe and trust he was God's ambassador in judgment and power; yet I doubted.

I knew there was only one hope. I must go to confession, there to expose the secret workings of evil upon my soul. Then, in greatest sorrow, like sinking despair clutching at my heart, I knew I had offended God by not obeying and trusting my director to the utmost command of obedience.

---

27  The entire purpose of Cora's writings is made clear: through her writings, spread the *Mystical Humanity of Christ* and the hope of overcoming the Mormon heresy. Cora shows great trust as she continues her spiritual journey in spite of having many doubts and fears.

*January 31 1947*

I made my confession and left the confessional with renewed hope and courage and with a peace that I have seldom felt or understood.

Two hours after the confession, I felt my soul drawn away into a spiritual embrace of love,[28] there to experience new delights and joys, which the world doth not understand. My soul, returning to the sensible understanding and knowledge that I had been with Jesus, remembered in the essence of knowledge I had promised Jesus I would try to overcome fear and, with His help, I would pray for the souls hidden in darkness through the western heresy.

Instantly I was again on the brink of the dark valley of death. Blackness was now a dull grey, which made it possible for me to [discern] the grey outline of the Mormon temple in a desert of awful loneliness. There before me stood our Blessed Mother near the ledge where the priest had instructed me to call on our Mother's tears to flood away the terrible heresy (demons in the form of black snakes). She was arrayed in a glistening white gown and in her hand reposed a blue rosary. Her beautiful fingers gently touched each bead, and as she prayed, it seemed as if a snowstorm of glistening white crystals floated around her in countless circles, thus enclosing her in a cloud of shimmering mists. The snowflake crystals showered on the earth at her feet. She asked me to gather them.

I knelt at her feet, and into a small bucket which lay on the ground, I gathered the little snowflake petals of holy grace. When the bucket was filled, she asked me to pour the contents into the dark valley. I walked to the edge of the valley and did as I was commanded. There I stood watching the snowflake particles scattering over the dark crevices on the steep slope of the valley. As I watched their little light fall into such great darkness, I grew afraid with the thought that it would be impossible to fill the great valley with graces if poured from such a small bucket.

I hurried to our Blessed Mother's side, there to inform her of my fear and to ask her for my release from such a mission. Before I could petition her, she spoke to me these words, "Refill the small bucket, and empty it again and again into the valley."

28  Ecstasy

I obeyed her request and, as I poured the second bucket of graces into the semi-darkness, I felt again the terrible despair and utter uselessness of such a mission. I again walked toward her to tell her of my fears, but she kindly informed me to gather the graces again. As I knelt before her to refill the small bucket, I felt our Jesus hurrying toward us. He quickly knelt beside me and said, "Here, let Me help you refill the bucket."

I walked with Jesus to the ledge, and He poured the contents of the bucket into the valley. I noticed His ease, composure, and willingness to try to fill the valley, even if it did seem a useless gesture. As we walked toward our Blessed Mother, Jesus said, "I don't understand why you are so frightened at the valley. On Good Friday, I'll traverse the complete depths for your people. Will your frightened heart still the desire of My heart?"

My soul instantly fled to Him, there to dissolve for a moment into the warmth of His hidden love. There I knew I asked to travel the depths for Him alone on Good Friday. I felt His heart was stilled in the inner peace in my heart.

It seemed as if in reward for my little willingness to please our Master, He told me He would be with me for about five hours on the fifth of February with further instructions and preparations for Good Friday.

*February 5 1947*
Near the hour of 6:00 p.m., my doctor and his wife, Mary (Jessie),[29] called on me for a visit. During the visit, I offered to read the writings on our Blessed Mother's hidden sorrow. As I began to arrange the papers, there above me appeared thousands of angels, all dressed in beautiful flowing gowns in pastel shades and hues, all in human forms of young men. They seated themselves in perfect order in a semicircle of golden chairs, which filled the heavens from the eastern skyline to the distant western darkness. In the essence of knowledge, I understood they were going to listen to me read the paper on our Mother's sorrow. I could hardly read the paper. I was stunned with the thought of such an audience, an audience of angels listening to mere human

---

29  *Dr. John J. McDevitt, M.D. and Mary Parrish McDevitt*, sister of *Father Frank Parrish, S.J.*; parents of *Michael McDevitt*, custodian for the writings of Cora Evans.

words of expression on Mary's sorrow. Their golden light, like the hot rays of the noonday sun, gave me the feeling of being sunburned. I wearied under the heavenly warmth, and I felt my heart racing as if racing with time and death.

As the reading was finished, I seemed to understand, as the heavenly vision dimmed before me, that I had in God's good grace given joy to the angels. They seemed to marvel that God's gifts were so clearly caught up into my soul, there to write them for His glory for souls on earth. As I folded the paper as one closing a book, my soul was again caught up into the heart of Jesus, and there we walked in the dusk on the ledge of the great dark valley. Jesus was dressed in a flowing green colored cape (lightly touched with purple) and embroidered with silver threads. His crosier was jeweled in green emeralds, rubies, and diamonds. Jesus handed me His crosier, but its weight was impossible for me to lift and there we stood gazing upon the symbol (crosier) of power, which I knew I must carry on Good Friday into the depths of the western heresy for Jesus.

> *"They seemed to marvel that God's gifts were so clearly caught up into my soul, there to write them for His glory for souls on earth."*

Jesus picked up the crosier and placed it lengthwise across my outstretched arms. In this way I was to carry His crosier into the dreadful darkness of death on Good Friday. My eyes followed His eyes into the valley of darkness, as He seemed to be mapping my future course into the threading gloom for souls. The distance seemed long and frightening to my soul. Then Jesus spoke, as my eyes fell upon the doors of the temple. "Cora, you will walk three times around the temple in honor of the Holy Trinity and each time with My crosier, mark the Sign of the Cross upon the temple door. Hundreds of conversions will be made this coming year through your efforts and your obedience."

Jesus spoke with great kindness into my soul—as if to try to erase the fearful thought of Good Friday—these words, "Your friends, Dr. Jack, Mary, and Edythe (my nurse), are anxious over you. Return to them and after a while, I'll take you to My heart again."

To this request I answered Jesus in great pain, for bodily senses were beginning to reawaken from their sleep of repose in God, "I don't want to return. Please don't let me return. Let me stay with You, my Jesus. Let me travel the valley of darkness this hour for You. Then perhaps I can stay with You always."

To this request of pain, Jesus answered kindly (trying again to reawaken my earthly mind to the gifts on earth), "Cora, your rosary sleepeth."

As Jesus spoke those beautiful sentiments of love toward the rosary into my soul, I noticed He held in His hand my little brown rosary.[30] Each bead appeared as a tiny sleeping bird huddled closely to the silver chain of love. Jesus touched a bead on the rosary and began to pray the Hail Mary prayer, and as He did so, the tiny brown bird awakened, fluttered its tiny wings, and flew away into the Eternal Father's light above us. As each prayer ended, the tiny birds flew away until the chain was empty with the exceptions of the larger beads, which did not resemble a tiny bird in symbolic meaning. As I opened my hand for Jesus to give me my rosary beads, I noticed in His hand was nestled another chain of sleeping birds. As Jesus handed me my rosary, He lifted His crosier from my outstretched arms, and we walked together as if back into the path leading to earth. I began to pray the rosary to please Jesus, but deep within my soul I was longing for death in Him, and so the tiny little brown bird just fluttered into the air and quickly returned to sleep again on the silver chain. I touched the next little bird and prayed with added interest and that little bird flew into a greater distance, but alas—it too returned to sleep on the rosary chain.

Jesus said, "Pray harder."

The next little brown bird was touched and prayed with more fervor, and it quickly left the chain of love to fly higher and higher into the far heavens never to return, for its purpose was with the Eternal Father. I sensed a feeling of joy—joy, the fruit of obedience.

My eyes opened on the smiling faces of Dr. Jack; Mary, his wife; and Edythe, who so graciously understood my mission of sorrow and joys. Jesus spoke into my heart, without the vision of Himself before me, these words, "I'll send Father Frank to you. He will help you carry the

---

30  On August 2, 2009, Cora's daughter, *Dorothy Evans*, presented the rosary as a gift to *Michael McDevitt*.

crosier into the valley of darkness. He will know and give the hour."

I visited with my friends for several minutes. I told them the beautiful story of the little brown birds and the second visitation, which would come soon.

Again I felt my soul taken away into His beautiful light as Father Frank and Mack entered the room. I saw them and spoke to them as if through a cloud of white smoke and then my soul was completely lifted from this earth into His embrace of love.

Later, as earthly senses began to reawaken themselves to the essence of earthly knowledge, I saw myself carrying the crosier on my outstretched arms as in the previous vision; however, I felt pleased as well as startled in the knowledge that the crosier felt light in its weight. A thought of joy flooded my soul that perhaps my cross would be lighter on Good Friday—lighter and with less fear, better to follow the course of steps the Master had charted for me.

Suddenly the crosier was heavier again, heavier than at any moment before. I felt myself bending beneath its weight, and in fear I looked up to find our Jesus and to beg His merciful help. There before me stood Father Frank, dressed in our Lord's cape of white and holding the crosier. I was astonished to find it was as light as a feather as long as I kept my soul's eyes on the cape of authority that Father Frank wore. I felt Father's blessings many times, and my soul was flooded with terrible remorse for ever having the slightest doubt in Father's judgment regarding my soul. Indeed he is God's ambassador of trust and faith.

Immediately to the left of Father Frank, still dressed in our Lord's cape of trust, stood our wonderful Jesus. Again I pleaded to be released to go with Him. Again I reminded Jesus I would be willing to travel the darkness in the valley if He would only take me to Him this day.

His look was one of sadness and again I felt the coursing, inconsolable grief within my soul. "I cannot leave You, Jesus. I cannot leave You," was all I could say.

Jesus sat down beside me and said, "If I take you with Me now, you will have less glory with Me forever." To this answer I seemed to shout as one in uncontrollable grief, "I do not want Heaven, nor any part of it. I only want to be a speck of dust clinging to Your sandal."

Our Jesus with tear-filled eyes whispered to me, "I do not like to leave you like this. Will you only trust Me? I know what is best for you," and then, as if to interest me in something of earth, He gently reawakened the thought of my friends to my earthly mind by saying, "You love Jessie, too, don't you? Dr. Jack would be surprised to see his halo. Ask Dr. Jack to leave you a stimulant. You will reach a very low ebb tonight. I trust Edythe with all your gifts. Now I bless all your personal friends. Will you now return to give My love and devotion to them?" I nodded I would. Jesus then handed me the crosier. It was very light in weight and for a second I experienced great joy and love, joy to better please Jesus above everything else.

Jesus then asked me to step down two steps into the valley of darkness. There I would stand in spirit with His crosier until Good Friday or until Father Frank gave me further instructions. As my eyes opened to the earth again, I heard Jesus repeating, over and over again, one word: "Write, write, write."

*I heard Jesus repeating, over and over again, one word: "Write, write, write."*

*Excerpt from "Spiritual Communion" (1944)*
In the holy hour of quiet prayer within the twilight of Thy beautiful light in meditation's path, I have at last found Thee, my Jesus. Tremulously, my soul breathes its way of love to Thee, and now in the sweet immersion of Thy beckoning love, I kneel before Thee, my Jesus, as Thou dost hang in majesty upon Thy cross. My soul cries out to Thee—how can I thank Thee for suffering for me? How can I show my appreciation for Thy great gift of faith given me in the hour of my conversion to Thee and Thy holy institution? O teach me, Beloved, how to teach and prove for Thy creatures who know Thee not, that Thou dost really live. Oh Jesus, help me. As my soul ventured nearer and deeper into His way of love in the quiet hour of prayer, I was permitted for an instant to gaze into His magnificent eyes where beauty, vastness, and knowledge are the essence of one meaning: His Love. Jesus spoke into my soul these words, as His right arm seemed to lift itself from off the cross to encircle my trembling body, "Make the chain longer." I seemed to be dissolved into a veil-like, soothing, liquid fire where

appealing grace in God's joyousness breathes in unbroken affections upon all who enter there. Hidden in the Sacred Wound of love in His side, I received our Blessed Lord in the form of the Little White Host. It fluttered like a wounded dove against my heart as though it were pleading for mercy to be awakened within my soul to better teach His countless souls on earth the meaning and understanding of His Sacred Humanity. As I began to leave the welcoming love of the Holy Wound, I heard Jesus speak again, "Make the human chain of My Humanity in souls longer and longer." I understood in spirit that our Blessed Lord desired us to receive Him often through the day and night in a spiritual Communion. Through receiving Him in an act of love, we would become like another soul to join the long human chain of another Christ's Humanity dwelling amongst us.

> ### As I began to leave the welcoming love of the Holy Wound, I heard Jesus speak again, "Make the human chain of My Humanity in souls longer and longer."

*Excerpt from "Jesuit Necklace" (1945)*
Oh my beloved Jesus, bless Thy holy priests, the Jesuits. Keep them free from sin. Especially bless Father Parrish. Bless him with Thy grace of love, better for him to be Thy faithful imitator. Bless his every footstep and each heartbeat with Thy song of love, "I love thee truly." Hourly embrace him in Thy shroud of perfect peace and imprint upon his soul thy glowing grace of love flowing from Thy Holy Wounds. Sanctify his every word, look, and gesture for he is Thy image, Thy earthly priest, and keeper of Thy prison home.

*Excerpt from "Skies' Cathedral and Father Parrish" (1945)*
Oh hour of solemn quietude in the Holy Mass, how can I welcome thee? Oh hour of the holy Voice of inspiration, take me away in Thy shroud of prayer into the city of vision in the joys of the skies' cathedral. Oh skies' cathedral, thou are our Blessed Mother's home and refuge of sinners, as well as those who love thee, Holy Mother and thy Son. Oh Blessed Mother, penetrate my soul with the longing to be in perfect union and love with thee forever and ever. Oh hour of sublime

love, adoration, peace, and worship, permit me to find through thee today a costly gem, a gift for Father Parrish, to show my appreciation and gratitude to him for his kindness to my wavering soul. For Father, I would choose a gift of beautiful light, a light that darkness cannot touch, a power of light to better shield him from the world's contagion as he tries in merciful charity to lift the many heavy crosses from weary souls. Permit, dear God, the gem to sparkle with grace of perfect quiet prayer wherein Father's words, deeds, and actions may lead him into a deeper dissolving love within the Sacred Host, our hidden God.

Down and through the great cathedral's silent corridors and silent winding paths, I prayed for the holy gift of deeper prayer for thee alone, Father Parrish. From a great balcony, I watched into the space of immensities where stood broad canyons, rolling meadows, tiny lakes, and rippling crystal streams, and there on a sloping hill, standing in the circle of a glowing crystal rosary, stood our Blessed Mother with her holy Infant Son cradled in her arms. As I asked for my petition for you, Father Parrish, our Blessed Mother smiled and from her eyes fell two tears. They splashed upon the crucifix on the rosary encircling her feet. I quickly knelt in reverence to kiss the holy tears and, as I knelt, I heard a sigh and prayer escaping from their crystal depths, "Atone, atone for the sins of youth." Her holy tears were shattered in a hundred fragments, covering the holy cross like a mist of dew, reverberating in a trembling way into incense which continually rose toward the cathedral's spires. Silently and in reverence, I gathered each fragment of the broken tears and kissed them one by one, placing them into a golden chalice which our Blessed Mother held close to her heart instead of her Infant Son. The ruby glow of our Savior's Sacred Blood within the chalice cast its shadows toward an altar where you, Father Parrish, offered sacrifice for love and penance for the world and its youth. As you lifted your eyes toward Heaven, your crown's inscription read, "Youth's pardon in sacrifice," and again I heard the deep melodious sigh from our Blessed Mother's soul, "Atone, atone for youth." She whispered into your soul, Father, as she handed you the chalice containing her precious tears mixed with Her Son's divine Blood.

*Excerpt from "Jesus Writes in Greek and Latin" (1946)*

One early morning during vigil hour to adore our Blessed Lord, I felt within my soul His blessed nearness and, for a moment while in adoration to Jesus, I felt I was no longer a divided heart in the path of distractions between God and earth, but solely alone with Jesus. Alone I dwelt with Jesus in His possession of immeasurable love where transcend His affections and consolations to souls who try to love Him.

There, within His holy grace of exquisite delights, I was permitted in spirit to watch Jesus writing with a pen upon two sheets of paper. The language[s] written on each paper differed in their characters, but I seemed to realize the message had the same meaning. I guessed, as one would guess in an earthly sense, the one language was Latin and the other Greek.

Jesus said to me as I knelt at His knee, "Receive ye permission to read them."

The following week I obtained the desired permission from my director, but I hesitated asking Jesus for the hidden meaning written on the two slips of paper, from January 1946 until Good Friday 1946, because of my unworthiness and wanting to prove to myself that I was not seeking knowledge out of curiosity.

Early Good Friday morning during another blessed vigil hour, it seemed I was given the privilege to kneel in spirit near our Jesus in the Garden of Gethsemane. There in the stillness of night, the solitude of His quiet way in the illumination of seraphs' glory and light, where constantly transcend the Eternal Father's gifts in wisdom, understanding, and love, Jesus and I talked to each other.

Now my soul cries in defeat as I try to recall into words the wondrous moment in Gethsemane. My soul seemed to [delight] to the nothingness of myself [and spoke] these words, "Oh hour of sublime beauty, oh hour of sublimest sentiments, how can worldly mind comprehend His magnificent voice and the gaze of His sorrowful eyes? Oh my soul, it seems thou hast failed me, for mere words cannot recapture one tone of His voice, nor is there one word to describe His tears. Oh hour of sublime magnificence, would that I could leave you as a sleeping child in death to remain forever undisturbed, but it is the will of holy obedience that I try to recapture for my friends the dust of knowledge hidden beneath the Master's feet."

There, in the captivity of His world where human speech is unknown, I understood it was our Beloved's desire to give me the knowledge and understanding of His letters written in Latin and Greek.

A moment later, within the embrace of His love, I understood Jesus to say, "Latin is My symbol for the universal language. Greek is the language known by few. It is the symbol of the spiritual life in Me. For the world to know Me as I desire to be known, the Greek language, or hidden spiritual life in Me, must be translated into everyday, universal language using words of simplicity, joy, and love.

*If My creatures would only take Me into their souls*
*and ask Me to be their constant companion,*
*much of earth's evils would cease.*

"My desire is to be a constant companion in the souls of My friends and, unless they receive Me in the Eucharistic bread, where I am in Person, I cannot be their constant companion except in memory or desire. I desire My creatures to know that I am real and I am a lonesome God on earth because my Humanity is not known, or believed, or lived. Yet every generation has heard My song, 'My delights are to be with the children of men.'

"If My creatures would only take Me into their souls and ask Me to be their constant companion, much of earth's evils would cease. The taverns of vice would close for shame because My companions would refuse to take Me into places of sin. Instead of places of sin, My companions would choose for me wholesome entertainment.

"My creatures fail to understand: they are a living chalice, the chalice or real home of the Holy Ghost. And that living chalice was blessed and consecrated with the greatest care and devotion, even greater than the golden chalice used in the Holy Mass. But alas, those same children take their holy bodies into the dens of evil, there to become soiled, bruised, broken, and even spit upon. I ask them, would they not hide in shame? Would they not make great acts of love in reparation, and would they not fight as for life if they, in those dreadful moments in places of sin, should chance upon a holy priest with chalice in hand walk into a tavern of evil and at the bar drink unto himself a toast in the midst of cursing, drunkenness, and lust? Yet I say, that golden chalice in the priest's hand is not real. It, too, will die with the world, but My chalices, the human body, will never die, for they are blessed and consecrated tabernacles, homes for the Holy Ghost.

The Holy Ghost hidden in His human chalice is always accompanied by thousands of holy angels. Oh My humble servant, tell My creatures to be thoughtful and careful where they take the Holy Ghost, for often, in and through those places of sin and desecration to His holy home (the human body), the Holy Ghost pleads with the Eternal Father to open the doors of justice upon the earth. Justice would and could consume the world with vengeance but, through willing souls who have taken Me into their souls, through them I plead for Mercy to the Eternal Father. And the light of My Resurrection in souls stays the hand of the Eternal Father, and justice turns its million eyes away from earth."

I heard my soul praying as I left our Savior's side in Gethsemane, and, with fear and trembling yet firm resolve, I promised to teach the real, living Jesus, the real, Human God-Man amongst us. As Heaven's light and understanding wavered before me, leaving me alone on earth, I fell into deeper prayer and sighed this prayer to the divine memory of His sublime goodness, to teach us His hidden life, his wish to make His life understood by all, His desire to live within us His divine life: "Oh radiant heights of love, Thou are purity and through the purity of intention and purity of real life, we live again for Jesus, live for His joy, live for His love, live to die with Jesus. Oh purity of soul, help me die to self when I again live in His possession of immeasurable love, where transcend His affections and consolations. Oh Jesus, take Thou all my will, my love and devotion to make Thee more alive in my humanity which I now give to Thee for Thee to purify and then to live within."

*Excerpt from "Mystical Humanity Foundation: Heart of Vigil Lights—His Friends" (January 18, 1947, Feast of Saint Peter's Chair)*
Hidden within the depths of myself, I placed myself in imaginary vision before Jesus in His tabernacle home. There in God's beautiful immersion for souls who love Him above everything else on earth, He

gave me the grace of hidden pain, a pain of inconsolable sorrow, the knowledge of our captive state (souls' restrictions within the confines of the clay body).

In the realities of the soul beyond the powers of the earth, I heard the gentle rustle of our Lord's robes of heavy silks. Suddenly it seemed as though I were kneeling before a communion rail in a foreign church not to the liking of my earthly memory. Jesus seemed to be tiptoeing toward me. His gestures, smile, and calm footsteps gave homage to the quietness and solemnity of His church. In front of me where I knelt and directly back of the communion rail stood a large, heart-shaped candelabra filled with unlighted [votive] cups in the cheerful colors of blue, gold, green, and red.

Jesus smiled at me as He lit a long taper with which to light, one by one, the vigil lights in the candelabra. As He set afire each candle, He gave it a name—names of my closest friends, and then He knelt beside me and we watched with the awe of reverence the little tongues of fire. They flickered as though speaking in a symbolic [language] about a desire of unwavering love for Jesus. Then, through the grace of God, I realized I was listening and watching the combined love of souls for a common purpose, a solemnization of authority and power for God and His desire through the union of souls as one for Him.

Jesus arose to His feet and spoke these words as He seemed to gaze in raptures upon the symbol of souls, "May the sublime calling of the Eternal Father bless each soul here represented with the grace of eternal love. Through them may His eternal love be manifested in and through each of their actions, words, and deeds. May their cloak of wisdom be a constant guide to a living motto, 'All for God's glory.' May each word, action, and deed remind them of humility, kindness, and charity as if the whole world depended upon their actions for the moment, lest perhaps the earth dissolve into nothingness because of their fault through unfaithfulness to God. [May] their love and devotion to My Humanity [be] the fires and pillars of strength in the foundation to the world's last devotion, in the world's last half hour, My Mystical Humanity."

Jesus walked around the end of the communion rail and stood facing the burning candelabra. There He seemed to embrace the burning heart of love and, as He walked backwards toward His tabernacle home, He carried the heart of love with Him. There in the great distance, the flaming heart grew smaller until it reminded me of an emblem of His love pinned over His Sacred Heart.

Before the holy vision dimmed before my soul's eyes, I was permitted to see each light burning brightly in the tiniest miniature vigil lights over His heart, and Jesus spoke with the greatest of love and devotion these words, "The holy oil will never diminish as long as thoughts of love feed the tiny tongues of fires. Each flickering tongue is the symbol of tongues speaking of love of Me or neighbor."

During my vigil with Jesus on February 7, 1947, I saw our Blessed Lord appearing to me as He had left me on January 18. He was wearing the tiny heart of vigil lights. They were beautiful in their holy light and appeared more beautiful than before. Through an embrace of love, Jesus permitted me to gather bits of knowledge as fragments of love for my friends on earth, and the fragments told me how on January 18 when our Lord appeared before the holy courts of Heaven wearing earth's holy emblem, earth's fires of love, all the angels and saints had received great pleasure. Their rejoicing was very [majestic] in its grandeur of understanding, for the lighted fires of His heart taught them one thing—the beginning of earth's last devotion, Christ's humanity among men, in the earth's last half hour of time. The pillar of strength had been accepted and loved by the Eternal Father and now that desire of all saints and angels was about to materialize. Earthly time was now in its last half hour of existence and then sin would be no more, and potters' clay would hold no more the hidden life of limitations.

*Excerpt from "Loneliness in Inexpressible Darkness" (1947)*
Oh, inexpressible darkness, thou are incomprehensible in thy depths of loneliness when Jesus has gone away for a little while. Little by little thou art even transported into my memory, and consciousness is saddened because thou, Oh loneliness, hast cooled the flame of love in my soul through longing, waiting, and watching for Him.

Yet I know, oh inexpressible darkness, thou are deliciously sweet and kind if I would but cease my foolish struggling and whisper quietly, "Jesus, I know Thou art here, for even in darkness Thou art present."

Oh embraceable love, for just a moment draw me to Thy affections and reestablish my former love, better to follow Thee as one entranced, not knowing darkness from light, nor light from darkness, but as an infant of complete dependability, not knowing nor caring whether I go.

From out of radiant darkness, my beloved Jesus drew near to my soul. From the abyss of ravishing light in an elegance of a hundred exquisite lights, as if each color were a glowing furnace afire, there glowed alone in the darkness the Jesuit necklace of perfect diamonds.

My soul cried aloud, "I know He is here for He wears them. I know He is here for He loves them. I know He is here for He is always with them. Oh, Jesus, Thou art here, yet I am blind to the splendors Thou would show me for I am like thorny thistles caught on Thy golden slippers. Oh, Jesus, teach me through the Jesuit furnace of love to love the sweet fragrance of night, to love the hidden melodies of Thy heart in the night of a soul, for Thou art there in light and in darkness, desolation, and bliss. They are all alike to Thee, for Thou art everywhere, my God."

Then to my soul I cried, "Oh, soul, why art thou sad? Dost thou not know through love and obedience in the diamond furnaces on earth He is there, hidden in each furnace of bliss on earth?"

*Excerpt from "Bridge of Meditation into His Heart"*
Suggestion: Read as a reflection in the presence of the Blessed Sacrament.

Rest and sleep in Him, oh soul of mine. Rest in holy rest in this thy hour of prayer with Jesus. Oh, soul, how sweet and sublime are the captivated wonders He joyously shows thee.

My soul cried, "Jesus, my beloved, all these gifts and holy wonders which Thou dost show me leave me fearful lest I may forget them. For when they are breathed in the breath and tone of earthly words, Thy sublime gifts seem like mere fantasies. Yet I know in the world of meditation, fantasy in earthly terms is beauty. Therefore, through sensible reasoning, fantasy is real, for all good thoughts come from Thee. Reasoning in the world of meditation makes fantasy or beauty beyond imagination. They, beauty in Thy thoughts, become the steps in meditation delights for souls better to climb in their quest for Thee in Thy Humanity.

"Souls thus in search of Thee, my Jesus, step quietly and surely upon the great bridge of meditation which leads from their hearts into Thy immensities. There, hidden in Thy immensities of knowledge, the body sighs as though dying because of beauty and its sublime understanding in Thee, through Thy reflections on the body through the hidden soul. Souls thus engaged on the bridge of sighs walk on and on until they feel lost as if they were nothing in Thy immensities. Yet soul breathes on because of enjoyment in Thy sublime gifts, oh my Jesus of wondrous charity."

There at once it seemed I stood upon an endless bridge, a bridge with its beginning in my heart, better to fashion for my delights an endless chain of steps leading, I knew, into the light of God. Each step reminded me of a closed book or a day in my earthly life. As I stepped upon one and then another, I heard whispered voices of praise and melodies telling me of virtues well practiced in the days gone by in my life. I walked on and on, step by step, listening to God's way of hidden delights and melodies, and from them I learned the greater need of prayer and courage to overcome selfish faults which sounded to my soul as hushed notes and only told me of neglect. A few books or steps were silent, and well I remembered they were the days of neglect of my Jesus. They were silent days telling me of searching for joys on earth above my Jesus. Other steps or books chimed like a thousand bells ringing in a joyous mood, and I understood they were the tones of angels' praise to God and which would last for all eternity in praise for my poor soul because it had tried to win a victory over sin.

My soul seemed to bend and weep over my sad neglect in the past years, and in bitter sorrow I gazed heavenward, better to say, "Forgive me," and there, walking toward me on the bridge of sighs, was our wonderful Jesus.

Suddenly I watched my own soul reflect its sinful, dimmed light upon the mirrored brightness of our Jesus in His sacred Humanity. His tender gaze and assurance of love in His embrace of understanding gave me courage to gaze upon my sinful self as if hidden in His light, and I breathed aloud, "Oh, merciful Jesus, burn away my sins. Burn away my body. Burn away my soul and let me live in Thee. Content I'll never be until I am with Thee, through Thee, and in Thee. Oh, mirrored brightness, hide me in Thy light. Hide my sinful soul beneath thy feet, there forever my delight will be complete."

My soul before His brightness dimmed into a mere shadow near His sacred Humanity, and I sensed these earthly thoughts as if He were allowing me to remember them as lessons for myself and friends. What do I say when near Him on the bridge of sighs? My reason seemed to answer me as if it were a living essence apart from my soul in this manner of reasoning, "With Jesus I need say nothing, for He is everything, all-powerful, and filling every need, care, and mood, for He knows our least desires. Even understanding is a useless essence and unnecessary in the immersion of love with Jesus. For in that great dissolving, even for a moment whilst souls live yet on earth, understanding is like a released bird from a cage. Neither does it first hesitate to wonder to where it shall fly, but it flies in joyous release into the exquisite freedom where beauty, music, and eternal truths mingle as one knowledge and where restrictions are never felt, never known."

My soul deeply hidden in His beautiful light asked, "Jesus, my beloved, if it is Thy will for souls better to understand true flight to Thee after they have tried to conquer self through sense mortification and obedience to Thee and to the laws of their chosen vocations in life, how may they find Thee in the greater heights of love on the bridge of sighs?"

Jesus answered, "It is I who call souls to the greater light of knowledge, either in real death or sleep of repose through meditation. I have promised to a few souls on earth a foretaste of Heaven, and to those souls who have tried to make perfect their wills in Me through self-mortification and who have tasted the delights of knowledge through meditation upon My life and spoken word, I breathe My gifts as I venture upon the bridge which leads Me into their hearts. Thus in their hidden prayer of repose for Me, I am enthroned for a second, while in other souls I am enthroned for days and years. These souls I often beckon to leave their own hearts and come to meet Me upon the bridge of sighs made beautiful by detachment to the world for love of Me. The bridge of sighs is rightly named, for indeed the body sighs in its union with its God and— knowing it must leave the sanctuary of delight for its earth mission—the soul weeps and the body sighs as though dying from a broken heart. Living death to these souls strikes hourly, and hourly they allow Me to resurrect in and through them, thus allowing Me to borrow their body as a mystical body for My delights, better to give the world My graces of love. These generous souls are My delight on earth.

"My first inner call is to souls thus entering upon the bridge of sighs in the world of higher meditation, where they forget their own existence and thus in souls' repose fly into My arms. I permit them to feel the hidden warmth of My love (knowing I am near) and to sense deeper love. These graces thrive though love into a love above everything else on earth, a love wherein worded prayers seem useless. Petitions seem troublesome, and true trust in the one thought of perfect love covers all the desires of worded prayers of praise, glory, thanksgiving, and petition. In the sleep of hidden repose, love alone understands love. Love thus in repose is the essence of God, for God is the higher and all love above everything else.

"When souls thus tastes this holy love, I give them the sleep of souls' repose, where for a moment or perhaps hours I find personal rest and comfort as you often experience in the calm, quiet rest in a church alone with Me as your silent Guest. Upon souls in the sleep of repose where only love is understood, I pour My greatest graces upon them. They are My living fountains of grace to the world. A soul thus lost in the quiet of love does not completely withdraw from the earth in all its natural senses, for the essence of knowledge cannot be quieted even on the holy way of meditation. Essence of knowledge thus causes souls to realize they are with Me, either in an embrace of their nothingness or as the receiver of knowledge that cannot be erased from souls' minds thus entrusted with the divine mission of forming earthly words to a reality which does not touch the senses as in true earthly adventures. The embrace of nothingness of self or partial dissolving in God is a complete nothingness for a moment, and that moment cannot be understood nor remembered in the slightest degree after repose of sleep in God. The essence of knowledge, even in a dimmed degree before Me, causes souls to realize love and so, in the sleep of repose, mind is not a silent void but rather it is love based on knowledge. Thus knowledge leads souls unmarred to the bridge where I meet all souls either in real death or in the essence of sleep in death whilst they sojourn on earth."

I heard my soul repeating these words of prayer as I walked alone, retracing my steps over the bridge of love, "Oh wondrous God, enrich our lives with the knowledge of Thee in Thy Humanity. For through Thee our path to Thee is easy. Death is sweet because we know how to reach our souls to Thee through prayer. Thus we are never alone. Help us to remember Thy wish, 'My delights are to be with the children of men,' and help us to make our delights on earth Thy delight. I love Thee, Jesus."

*Excerpt from "Colors of the Universe"*
My weekly confession ended, and with a lightsome heart I left the sacred hall of justice (the confessional) and like anew, my soul seemed to wear as an emblem the kind words from my confessor's lips. Words there placed were never to be erased, for they had touched my soul with new light, hope, and understanding in the tender mercies of God.

Into dark depths of disappointment I had fallen because I had felt disheartened in what I thought were futile efforts and attempts to love Jesus and have others love Him as the divine, human friend and God to all. As I walked nearer to God's tabernacle home on the altar, with a prayer of thanksgiving in my heart, I felt our Beloved's embrace of love, and there it seemed I fell asleep in His arms as a tiny child. Asleep in meditation's prayer, I was graced with vision's knowledge to understand (in a tiny degree) God's loneliness in His tabernacle prison for us sinners who neglect Him, our silent, willing Prisoner.

While thus praying in thanksgiving for the gift of His most chosen desire (the grace to console Jesus in His loneliness), meditation's whispered breath spoke into my sleeping soul these words, "Little soul in God, remember always with God there is no time."

## *I found myself as the infant listening to the beating of God's Sacred Heart.*

I found myself as the infant listening to the beating of God's Sacred Heart. Like gentle knocking upon a door, it seemed to be persistent in calm, quiet, and peace, to reverberate through my soul these words, "Plead with man to heed My inspirations."

I answered, "Dear Jesus, I believe through Thy grace Thy gifts are many and great and may be gained if we but open the door of our hearts to better heed Thy ever whispering voice and give ourselves to Thee." As my prayer ended, the altar and tabernacle before me faded away into the mist of meditation's time. There in the midst of heavenly tones of music, seen with the spiritual eye (tone as color and blending hues), stood our divine Shepherd clothed in a cope of red and gold over an ivory and blue gown. His sandals were gold and covered with jewels, matching in brilliance the tall golden crosier which He carried magnificently in His right hand. As Jesus walked slowly toward the communion rail where I knelt, He sang these words with a delightful air of happiness, "My delights are to be with the children of men."

. . . As Jesus sang His song, He walked slowly into meditation's path and there beside Him, I prayed alone these words, "Great Love, please give me the grace of perfect detachment, for it will take that grace to better leave the beautiful spectrums of green and violet and the many other shades in the great and terrible triangles of beautiful hidden mystery as a sacrifice of penance for my neglect of Thee, my Jesus, in the Blessed Sacrament. Please give me the grace to remember the vision and understanding in Thy wisdom to better relate to friends Thy hidden mystery of love for them when they reach their journey's end. Help me, Jesus, to write them as You would like them written for Thy glory to be better known among men. May Thy glory be glorified through my memory to write Thy wishes for the benefit of mortal souls who are held beneath the iron rule of prophets who find delight in their earthly strength in teaching a doctrine which embraces the broken Trinity."

. . . As I watched the earth in its great minuet design, my soul poured forth this prayer for my people, the Mormons, "Oh, my God and God of love, in Thy tender mercy, save my people. In Thy mercy Thou hast given me the grace of love of reparation for self and friends, and now I offer Thee the sacrifice of my meager will in thanksgiving for Thy tender mercy. Remember, Jesus, once I was Thy greatest care. Yes, I was Thy greatest sinner, and Thy tender gaze of mercy did save me. In Thy holy grace, my soul was permitted to kiss Thy sacred shroud and see in faith Thy glorious Self hidden in the lifted Host each day in the Holy Sacrifice of the Mass. I believe and trust in Thy mercy because I remember Thy holy words to the prophets of old, 'My hand is outstretched still.' Oh, hear my prayer in Thy kindness and grant my sacrifice of my will to be forever dissolved beneath Thy feet, there to be enwoven in Thy embracing love. Permit my soul in Thee and by Thee and through Thee to glorify God the Father by the repeated song of my people in the days to come, when they shall lift their hearts to Jesus in calling for the shroud of crucifixion in the form of the Living Bread.

. . . "Jesus," I sighed, as the holy vision dimmed away, "Have mercy on the souls who reject Thy grace of love and conversion. Help me with Thy grace of understanding and trust to write the vision and knowledge Thou hast entrusted to me for mortal souls to use to better gain true love of Thee. My soul gives Thee thanks for this great trust and, in that trust, I believe Thou will help me write the knowledge for souls to use as a stepping stone to love Thee more, and, dear God, please permit this knowledge through Thy grace to awaken a soul to Thee as he lingers near the brink of Hell."

. . . My soul cried out as Jesus smiled upon my nothingness, "Oh, my Jesus, Thy lingering smile, I cannot part with Thee. Would that I could this moment choose death to go with Thee. Oh, Jesus, mercy on my frailty and fear about the mission Thou has entrusted to me. Please with Thy grace to help me. Imprint Thy holy smile upon my memory as a pledge of trust in Thee. Oh, Jesus, what can I do for Thee?"

Jesus smiled, and with a slight bow He said, "You may give Me your eyes. Through earthly eyes I love to relive again. Through your eyes, I'll gaze into souls, there to imprint My love, My will, My trust they will follow Me."

*Excerpt from "Mystical Humanity"*
I remember well, dear Holy Spirit, in the depths of meditation's prayer, I was permitted to watch the holy hand of our beloved Jesus write these words with my pen, "It is thy duty and obligation to propagate My Mystical Humanity." Thou hast also asked me to be hidden from the world, whilst in another gift of deeper understanding, Thou didst show me a beautiful vision of Thyself upon the holy cross. And from that cross Thou didst lift Thy holy hand away from the piercing nail, and Thy arm embraced me to Thy bleeding Heart, and while I kissed Thy Sacred Wound of love, I felt a friend clasp my hand in his and, as I gazed upon that friend, his hand was clasped to another friend's hand, and so a living chain of friends was formed which seemed to encircle the earth and Thou, beloved Jesus, didst say into my soul, "Make the chain longer."

*Excerpt from "Another Christ (Our Priest)"*
Christ's ambassador[31], our priest, made his sick call visit to a friend. He blessed her and then sat down for a friendly visit. Her words of thanksgiving (the symbol of all mankind in praise and appreciation for a priest's kindness and visit of consolation) raised her thoughts to the love of God. While she was thus speaking her words of thanksgiving, her eyes glanced upon his priestly hands, those precious hands anointed for God, as they lay folded in his lap.

In God's beautiful way through grace, for souls to pray for the safety of His consecrated sons, she quickly found her way into the realm of a soul's death—into a world of burning, ardent love through meditation, where even memory fails to the delights of earth. For well she knew the meaning and power of those anointed hands and, in God's embrace of love, she wanted to pray for the preservation and safety for all God's anointed hands.

She spoke slowly and quietly in a rapture of love to the father beside her, "Father, I love to look at your hands. They are so blessed. They are living ciboriums. They held the Creator this morning. I am not worthy of this sublime privilege to gaze upon the visible hands of another Christ." Her eyes searched for the darkness of solitude, better to hide away from such a wondrous sight, and there, her spiritual eyes fell upon the scene of a thousand angels watching and venerating the august hands of the priest beside her. The song of veneration seemed to reverberate through her soul in this meaning, "Oh unmeasured love, oh unmeasured and incomprehensible bliss, we never weary with the sublime gift of admiration and love as we stand in awe before the shrine of anointed hands, the visible, living hands of another Christ on earth."

The angel spoke to the woman these words, "How blessed you are, oh mortal soul. You have not only looked upon those anointed hands but you have even dared to touch them when he greeted you. Do you know how blessed you are? Do you realize, oh body of clay, that you have touched Christ's divine nature through His holy grace of transfiguration in His other Christs, the priests on earth?

31  The priest referred to in this piece, written in the third person by Cora Evans, is *Father Frank Parrish, S.J.*, her spiritual director and confessor.

If we could envy you, this would be the reason. You have touched God's divine nature when you touch those anointed hands. When you touch them, we stand aghast and wonder how you feel when your hand breaks through the golden light which transcends those anointed hands. Do you feel in your flesh the experience of power and its vast unutterable wisdom proceeding from the divinity hidden in those anointed hands? Yes, we wonder how you dare to touch them and, when we see those hands open Heaven's fountains of grace upon creatures and ourselves, we bow in adoration and all Heaven trembles when those hands open Heaven through the holy Name of God. Oh, mortal soul, govern thyself in the paths of perfection, better to reverence and give glory to those anointed hands, the living ciboriums now before you."

. . . The woman's eyes gazed tenderly upon the priest's hands as they still lay folded in his lap and she said aloud, "Oh immortal, anointed hands in God's exquisite reflections and devotion to us, bless me and heal my sinful soul. Make me like unto the flaming image of God through the grace of transubstantiation, for your hands can do this, Father. You can break me into nothingness and in nothingness, like the symbol of bread; you may take me into the light of the unknown because you are another Christ on earth."

While yet in meditation's rapture, the woman asked God to bless the priest before her and, as the priest bowed his head to join his prayers with hers, there before her knelt not the priest, but the real Christ Himself. To the woman, Jesus spoke these words, "This priest's glory within Me is beyond explanation. His nature in Me cannot be comprehended for, inch by inch, he has found his way with Me, through me, and in Me. His complete immolation of will and self brings Me the pleasure of constant transfiguration in him. I am allowed this pleasure in only one [out] of My one thousand priests. I bless you through him, for him, and by him, for he is your will, the government of your soul, and the key to My eternal Kingdom for you."

*Excerpt from "Christmas Eve—1946: Jesus to Foster Mystical Humanity; Personal Angel of Christ"*
A few minutes later, our Jesus informed me He Himself would foster the world's last devotion, the Mystical Humanity within souls. He told

me I would be persecuted for His devotion but to remember always He could do all things, even to forgiving the greatest sins, and to remember that sometimes He has allowed the greatest sinners made new to open the greatest doors to Him. Jesus then looked to the holy angel and told him to dismount from the horse, leave the court of God's personal angels for the rest of finite time, and heed the prayers from souls who lived and fostered the Mystical Humanity devotion. Jesus prayed the first prayer as He would wish us to use to ask the care and protection from His angel in these words, "Oh, Angel from God's personal court of angels, guide and protect me for Jesus is within me in the Little White Host."

As the great angel heard the sublime words of prayer from Jesus, he bowed his head in the greatest of devotion and handed Jesus his silver gloves and walked away into the darkness of earth. Beautiful thunders from Heaven filled the earth with tidings of joy as the angel left the Light of his Creator. While the rumblings were offering praise, our Jesus spoke to me these words, "Tell Dad Hession, your good husband, and My prince, they equally share in the joys of your grace—'confirmed in grace.' I personally bless all your friends who have taken Me as their living companion within them hour by hour. My gift to them is My personal angel."

I knelt in thanksgiving for such a gift for my friends, and all I could say was, "I'm such a sinner. I'm such a sinner." Jesus answered me as I rose to my feet, "Yes, you are a little sinner, but your trust has made you whole again." As Jesus spoke thus, the question arose in my mind as to whom He referred to as His prince, for often He Himself is called Prince, and, as my mind was questioning His meaning, the thought came to me that He meant Father Frank, and as I thought about Father Frank, our Lord bowed His Head and smiled beautifully and again said, "My prince."

*"Oh, Angel from God's personal court of angels, guide and protect me for Jesus is within me in the Little White Host."*

Note: The following stories are excerpted from Cora's full-length book on the life of Christ, *The Refugee from Heaven.*

*Excerpt from* The Refugee from Heaven *(circa 1954)*
*Book One, Chapter One: The Nazarene*
An attractive, middle-aged woman and her small grandson walked slowly along the shores of Mount Carmel Bay and looked out anxiously across the rough waters of the Mediterranean Sea. Gently, yet firmly, the woman held fast to the boy's small, chubby hand as he tried to free himself to run with the receding surf that creamed white just beyond his feet. They were waiting and watching for the appearance of fishing ships on the far-distant horizon.

The boy tried to wrest his hand from hers and the woman said with a trace of sternness in her voice, "Not now, son. Another day you may chase the seabirds and race the surf. Now, we must watch and pray for your grandfather's safe return with his men and ships."

The boy asked, "How long will that be?"

"He should arrive before sundown," his grandmother answered. "Come, let us watch."

Within an hour several other women and children, as well as many aged and poor, assembled on the beach. Carefully they scanned the watery horizon for the waving banners of Simon's fishing fleet.

Simon was known throughout this land as the greatest captain of the sea. Although self-skilled in navigation, it was claimed he had never lost a ship. Nor had he ever turned away the poor when they asked for fish as he lay anchored in the bay. He always listened kindly to the oppressed and the afflicted and offered them words of counsel on faith and loyalty to God above and beyond their thoughts of self. He was strong, courageous, just, and charitable.

A faithful worshiper, he often prayed in the synagogues with his brother, Andrew. It was not at all uncommon to hear Simon praise Andrew's charitable prayers and sacrifices, for he believed those prayers to be direct channels of his good fortune in finding the best schools of fish in the rivers of the sea. Many people believed him wealthy for he owned the largest fishing fleet in that district. However, he was not, because of his excessive charity for the poor.

Suddenly, a joyous cry arose from the crowd. Black specks, tiny on that great waste of water, were Simon's fleet and they grew taller, inch by inch, as they slowly climbed the steps of the sea toward the dry land.

Presently one ship could be seen ahead of the others. It was Simon's and its great banners of crimson and gold waved high on the ocean's breeze. Eagerly those on shore listened to the deep tones of its great bell which told them that all was well. Faintly its sound carried to them above the crashing roar of the breakers.

Two hours later the ships anchored. Simon immediately leaped overboard and swam toward the shore where his wife and his grandson, hand in hand, stood ankle-deep in the frothing surf. He greeted them with most tender affection and together they waded to the dry land. All about them others were greeting their men also, as they swam in from the ships.

As Simon dried the seawater from his powerful arms and shoulders, Rosa Maria told him the news of the village. It was all very commonplace and uninteresting—except for the fact that he was expected to appear, even at this late hour, before the local Council of the Sanhedrin.

Simon's deep voice growled above the pounding of the waves and then subsided as he learned that he must defend one of his own fishermen. He was content then. Who else would protect his men if he, Simon, did not?

Sending his wife and his grandson on ahead to the village, Simon shouted orders to his fishermen and to the sailors still aboard the ships. Almost immediately great copper kettles, measuring some four feet across, appeared over the sides and were floated shoreward. As they drew nearer, other sailors grasped them and dragged them up upon the beach. They were filled to the brim with fish, Simon's present to the aged and the poor. He smiled contentedly as he watched them as they pushed forward, thanksgiving upon their lips.

As Simon started for Mount Carmel and the Sanhedrin, he noticed a tall, well-built Stranger reclining on the beach watching the scene with great interest. He seemed intrigued with the quick obedience given Simon by his men and by the calmness and the order with which the people emptied the great kettles.

As Simon approached, the Stranger arose and stood watching him. Simon wondered who He was and from where He might have come, for he was quite sure he had never seen Him before. Then his interest quickened and deepened beneath the impact of the calm dignity of this Man. As he drew nearer he could see His beautiful eyes quite clearly and that He was not a sailor for His magnificent hands were not thick and calloused. Yet He seemed intensely interested in the laborious work of the crew and in their care of the poor.

The Stranger smiled at Simon's expression of puzzlement. "Good evening, Captain of the Sea," He said quietly. "I have long looked forward to meeting you for I have heard much that is good about you. Your countrymen praise you highly for the discipline with which you govern your men. I must also praise them for their obedience to your least command. Such cheerfulness can only be the result of the justice and the charity of the man who captains them."

Simon stood quite still as though stunned. Never had he heard such a voice nor had he ever been so praised before. Most men remained silent in his presence, for was he not the Captain, and did not men out of respect wait for him to speak first? He asked, "Who are you, sir? Thank you for what you have said, but I am sure I do not deserve your praise."

The Stranger's voice was even more quiet than before as He answered, "I am Jesus of Nazareth. It is an honor, Captain, to speak with you."

As Simon opened his mouth to make reply, he was interrupted by shouts and commotion on board his ship. As he peered through the rays of the golden sun he could see two men lashing at each other with long, silver fish, using them as though they were swords.

Silent indignation flashed from Simon's eyes as he shouted a command to cease. The men did not hear him. Angrily, he then strode through the surf and swam quickly to the ship.

Grasping a low-hanging, knotted rope, he swung himself over the bow. Without questioning either fighter, he picked up one from the deck and hurled him into the sea. The other he ordered back to work. It was too bad the Stranger from Nazareth had seen that breach of discipline, but then he had handled it well enough.

Once more on shore Simon brushed sand and water from his feet and said, "I'm sorry about that disturbance, but it was easily taken care of. However, now I shall have to be going, for there is a matter in town which demands my attention. Good day, Sir, I hope I shall see you again."

He started away. He was filled with satisfaction over the way he had handled the fight and in the kind nod the Nazarene had given him. He was glad his countrymen respected him for his many virtues of justice and charity. It gave him a nice, warm feeling.

"Captain," the Nazarene said, "I know you are a man in favor of strict justice, and I was just wondering whether or not you threw the right man overboard?"

Simon came to a sudden stop. Had he been just? He hadn't allowed either man to explain what had happened. He suddenly became uneasily aware of rash judgment.

Without a glance at Jesus, Simon crossed the beach and once more plunged into the sea. When he reached his ship he climbed aboard, hand over hand. Finding the other offender, he quietly and without a word threw him over the side.

His crew looked at him in amazement. They had never before seen their captain in such hasty action, nor was he usually so easily angered. What in the world was the matter with him?

In answer to their questions Simon said, "I was profoundly disturbed with the thought that I had acted unwisely and unjustly toward the first offender by throwing him overboard while the second offender merely resumed his work. Now, I have treated them with equal justice."

He buffeted his way to shore. Once there he nodded cheerfully to Jesus as if to say, Sir, justice has now been carried out. You need worry no more about it.

"Are you sure, Captain," Jesus asked, as Simon once more started away, "that it was a fight, or was it simply boisterous fun among happy men?"

Simon froze as though brought abruptly to attention by a commanding officer. His pride now hurt, he began to wonder why he should be so questioned and disturbed by a Stranger. Turning to Jesus he asked in a tone of agitation, "Why are you, a Nazarene, concerned with what I do? And why do you ask about my men?"

Jesus answered calmly, "A man of justice is disturbed only when he feels guilty of an unjust act pertaining to a question involved at the moment. A just man has a fine conscience—so fine it cuts his soul with the fierceness of a flaming sword when justice is bruised. No one escapes it, for it wounds each man's soul according to the depth of his love for God."

He then extended His arms in blessing. "Simon," He continued, "be absorbed in God. His blessedness of joy, love, and charity are yours. Pray to be a fisherman of souls."

This strange blessing frightened Simon. Suddenly, however, he became aware of an interior feeling of subjection toward the Nazarene where before he had felt a growing animosity. He relaxed his fists at his sides and wondered what kind of power this Man had.

Without speaking, Simon returned again to his ship. He found the two offenders and demanded the reason for their fight. To his surprise he learned it had not been a fight at all, but a mimic duel in which the men had used fish instead of swords. When Simon heard this he swallowed a little and then apologized as he gave them permission to continue their sport.

This time he was not quick of step when he returned to shore. He was thinking deeply about what had happened and about the holy words of wisdom which the Stranger had spoken. He looked around quickly and discovered Jesus had left the shore and was walking along the path toward the village. He hurried to overtake Him.

When he reached Him and fell into step beside Him he said, "Jesus of Nazareth, are you a tradesman of spice and fine linen? If you are not, perhaps you are a master of wisdom and knowledge?"

"I am not a tradesman," Jesus answered. "In fact, I am a poor man. However, I am a teacher of the philosophy behind the New Law which is to teach you and everyone else on earth about the love of God."

Simon tried to hide his surprise. Surely this powerful-looking Man could not be a philosopher. Such men were usually frail and hidden in prayer in the synagogues.

He exclaimed, "You're joking with me! I need men like you, with good physiques and great knowledge, to man my ships. What do you say now? Be here tomorrow before dawn, and I'll hire you as my assistant."

Jesus said nothing, so Simon continued, "I would like to learn more of your wisdom concerning the new way of love for God, for we all expect the Messiah to arrive and dwell with us during this age, as you no doubt well know. However, we don't know just exactly when that will be."

Still Jesus did not say anything. Simon went on, "Work on my ship will be a good change for you. Perhaps you need to get away from the quiet life you must be accustomed to in Nazareth. In fact, if you come with me, you will get an enlightened view of the world and of the people who live about you. In mixing with them you will realize that the question uppermost in their minds is, when will the Messiah come? Your philosophy should be very useful to all of us after He has arrived. Do you happen to possess facts or figures as to when we might expect Him?"

Jesus smiled slightly as He answered, "I am not seeking work but I thank you very much for your kind offer. I choose to continue My search for wounded souls, for I can give them hope through the love of God and His mercy. His ways are those of merciful consolation, love, and hope for eternal life after death, since this life soon ends for all of us. I find great joy in doing this for it makes Me a physician of souls."

Simon marveled at this Man's words. More than ever he wished he could persuade Him to work on his ship. However, if He would not do that, perhaps He would tell his crew just what He had told him. Jesus promised to do as Simon wished the following evening.

The two men parted and as Simon hurried on into town he thought over what the Nazarene had taught him—especially about guarding against rash judgment, a fault he had failed to see in himself before.

He would have to tell Rosa Maria and Andrew, who lived with them, about this Jesus of Nazareth. He and Andrew had often discussed the coming of the Messiah (as indeed, who had not?), and they had often hoped they might be among the fortunate ones to live on earth when He did come. Anything new concerning Him was of great interest to both of them. Yes, he could hardly wait to tell Andrew about Jesus and about what He had said concerning God.

But first he would have to appear before the Sanhedrin in behalf of the man who needed him. He stepped forward cheerfully into the approaching dark and was soon lost to sight.

*Excerpt from* The Refugee from Heaven
*Book One, Chapter Two: The Nazarene Is Loved by the Crew*
Rosa Maria was preparing dinner for Simon and Andrew. She was a small, dark woman with large brown eyes that reflected the gentleness

of a lovely culture, and she wore her straight, black hair in two long braids heavily ornamented with strands of pearls. Because she was happy, she laughed with Andrew at her grandson who was romping with the dog. Yet she knew her brother-in-law was troubled, for she could not help but see how anxiously he watched down the night-filled pathway for the coming of Simon.

She asked quietly, "Are you still wondering whether or not to tell Simon about John?"

"It has been tremendously interesting watching him baptize hundreds of persons, Rosa," Andrew answered somberly, "and to listen to his teachings that his baptism is an outward penance for their sins, a penance that will make their souls pure in the eyes of God before the coming of the Messiah. Did you ever hear anything like that before?"

Rosa shook her head.

"That's just the trouble," Andrew went on. "Neither did anyone else that I know of. And that isn't all. From what he said, you might think the Messiah is already here on earth with us right now!"

Rosa gave a little gasp and stood very still. She asked, "Are you sure, Andrew? There have been so many impostors lately. Even though his actions are ceremonial and seemingly motivated by the most charitable principles, it is still possible that he is not what he seems . . ."

"That's why I'm reluctant to tell Simon about him," Andrew answered quickly. "Why, only a month ago Simon spoke with deep emotion of his soul's loneliness and his longing for the day when God would be with us. It would be cruel to raise his hopes by telling him what the baptizer says if it is false."Rosa asked, "Isn't there some way you can make sure?"

"I will pray and make inquiries." Andrew answered simply. "I may even question him, directly. Beyond that . . ."

For a few moments there was a deep silence in the room, broken only by the sound of the boy playing with the dog. The Messiah already on earth? Where? Could such a tremendous gift be possible? Wasn't it being presumptuous even to hope for it? Simon had said something like that once.

A bright, gentle light appeared in the depths of Rosa's eyes. She said at length, "I will pray with you, Andrew. What is the other name the baptizer gives to the Messiah?"

Andrew answered softly, "You mean, The Bridegroom?"

"It is a beautiful name," Rosa said slowly. "How could a man who speaks like that be very wrong in what he says?"

Simon came home triumphant, at last, from his appearance before the Sanhedrin, and as the four ate their dinner, he told them about his meeting with the Stranger on the beach that afternoon and of the episode on board his ship. They chuckled over his embarrassment and listened with interest as he even reenacted the mimic duel and confessed his humiliation when he realized his need for God's help and for self-control.

He intended telling them, also, the Nazarene's name and something of His philosophy, but he hesitated, for face to face with Andrew, he remembered how unbending he was in his respect for the old laws of Moses. He would have nothing at all to do with these self-styled teachers and preachers that seemed to be springing up everywhere these days. Yet, if one did not listen to them now and then and sift the evidence of their remarks carefully, how was one to know the truth? Simon decided not to tell Andrew any more than he had already. For that reason he did not ask him to attend the speech scheduled for the next night.

On his part, Andrew was surprised that Simon had paid the least attention to the Stranger. Could He have been John the Baptizer? If so, He must not have said anything about His doctrine of cleansing souls. For a moment, Andrew toyed with the idea and discarded it as being unlikely. However, John was an orator as well as a man of great wisdom . . . Andrew determined to listen closely to him the next time he spoke for any word that might correspond with what the Stranger on the beach had said.

The next night Andrew prayed silently in the synagogue for the grace of knowledge and wisdom to analyze John's statements correctly. From whom and from where did he receive the original principles which he taught?

Andrew felt that he must be a holy man, for it was claimed that he knew loneliness and hunger and had kept long vigils of prayer in the desert. It was also voiced through the land that he was alone in the world, that his relatives were as strangers to him, and that he cared little for current events. People said that his constant companions were pain, fasting, and penance. From all this it would seem that the unction of God must be upon his work, but in spite of it all Andrew still felt the need for further investigation.

On the beach, Simon, with forty of his men, awaited the arrival of the Nazarene. Driftwood fires were ablaze and towering peaks of fire, like golden tongues, cast a copper glow over the black, lapping waves as they rose and fell near the waiting men. Gone from the earth were the last rays of twilight and all was quiet except for the sound of the sea. Simon caught his breath in wonderment as the magnificence of a pale moon clothed the restless water in a majestic, shimmering gown of silver blackness that stretched as far as eye could see beyond the glow of the fires. Even the crew was caught and held in this great shroud of beauty.

Suddenly, Simon jumped to his feet. His quick ear had caught the sound of a footfall. Cupping his hands to his mouth he shouted, "Hello! Are You Jesus of Nazareth?"

The clear, calm answer came back to him, "Yes I am He. I am glad to be here with you, Captain."

Slowly, Jesus emerged from the shadows, and approaching the fires He said kindly, "Simon, may the same measure of peace and symbolic beauty which is in the evening world attain for you, through the Eternal Father, the grace to understand the unchanging truths of love and charity that souls have one for the other."

Simon felt the same awe before this Man that he had experienced the previous afternoon and again he was at a loss to understand it. Quietly he introduced Jesus as a philosopher and a carrier of good news concerning the Messiah's reign.

Jesus faced the semicircle of curious men. With the sighing of the sea in His ears and the fire casting flickering shadows across His face, He spoke to them.

"The ancient prophets," He said, "saw the God-Man in vision, and in this deep prayer of union, they were taken up into God's light where there is no time, and in that wisdom where everything is present, they walked and talked with Him."

He told them that the prophets had been deeply grieved when they learned how the Messiah would die—on a cross—because He was believed to be an impostor. He urged them to study the Scriptures and the words of the prophets so that they would know the Messiah when He came, and thus not have a hand in putting Him to death.

He told them of God's Heart on earth and how that Heart symbolized all truth and infinite love.

"The Sacred Flesh of the Messiah," He said, "will be the castle of the Eternal Father, and the God-Man will say, 'He who sees Me, sees the Father. He and I are One.'"

Jesus continued, "In all things except sin, the Messiah will be like you. Watch and pray so as to recognize Him, for He could be your closest friend. His Heart of fire, like this blazing fire before you, will win eternal life for you if you pray, study, and listen to His words which are given to you through the prophets.

"Through penance and prayer you will know Him, and the spiritual fire within you will become His other indwelling. Keep that fire burning—don't let it die as this driftwood fire burns away. You are as worthless pieces of driftwood without the effects of penance, and you are cast out upon a sea of pain and of strife. Our life here on earth is but a means of winning the reward of life everlasting. Win this life everlasting through penance and the love of one for another.

"The God-Man cannot die and His word is truth. Down through the ages and even to this hour He whispers, Come to Me! When you finally know Him, you will be symbolically washed ashore and He will enkindle you into the likeness of His Father. Driftwood either becomes waterlogged in the sea, which represents sin, or it washes ashore, there to dry in order to become another transformation. You will be a transformation without sin, which will make you clothed in transfiguration.

"Become brave in the goodness and the likeness of God while you live on earth. All of these things the Messiah will teach you in a greater way when you know Him. He will need brave men—men who are not afraid to expound to the world the brightness of His Fire within them."

Jesus told them more, but it all concerned eternal life and God's personal love for each and every one in the world. The driftwood fires at length smoldered into black ashes, and those rough men of the sea wished only one thing above all else on earth, namely: to find the God-Man and to follow Him. None of them had ever heard a man talk as Jesus had, nor say the things He said. From that hour on their lives were changed.

In their new love for God they pledged allegiance to their Creator to be as one in mind and to go in search of the Messiah no matter where He might be. Somehow, they now believed Him to be on earth.

Some of them thought Jesus an inspired prophet filled with wisdom and a gift of speech. Others wondered whether or not He might even be the Messiah, for He was to them as they would want the Messiah to be, a Man filled with understanding, kindness, and cheerfulness. Yet they did not dare ask Him. How they wished they were scholars of Scripture, for then they would know, as He had told them. They at length contented themselves by pleading with Him to visit them again and to tell them where they might begin their search for the Messiah and into what far lands they must travel.

Jesus answered by bowing His head and praying silently for them to receive the grace of faith. It was not yet time for Him to tell them who He was, for He wanted them first to have greater merit by searching for Him.

When He had gone, Simon dropped to his knees in the sand. One by one his men followed suit. They prayed that God would accept their pledge to search for the Messiah, and they pleaded with Him to make them His bodyguard, His providers, and the worshipers of His love. Eager to begin their search, they hoped God would chart their course so that success might at last be theirs.

Simon at length returned home. In answer to the question in Rosa's dark eyes, he took her into his confidence and enthusiastically told her of the wonderful talk Jesus had given and how he and his men had pledged themselves to leave all earthly possessions and careers and go in search of the Messiah.

Icy fingers plunged deep into Rosa's heart and then just as suddenly vanished. At that instant she was drawn into the same loving grace which God had given to Simon. She begged to be allowed to see and hear Jesus, too, the next time He spoke. Simon readily gave his permission but asked her to stay back out of sight. Rosa promised happily.

But, what to tell Andrew? For the time being Simon did not know, and he asked Rosa not to say anything to him about the incidents and the decisions of that night. Andrew was certain not to approve.

Rosa kept the secrets of both men deeply within her heart. She prayed constantly during the days that followed for God's guidance over them, for surely both could not be right.

A strange restlessness, coupled with a loneliness they did not understand, descended upon Simon and his men during the following week. They agreed that they missed the company of Jesus. But why should this be true of a man they had known only such a short time?

Finally, Simon decided to go in search of Him. He found Him in Mount Carmel talking to a group of men, explaining the views of the prophets on earthquakes, floods, and the end of the world. None of these questions and answers was of the slightest interest to Simon. All he wanted to hear and to learn was the New Law of Love, and how he could begin his search for the Messiah. He firmly believed that such a man of wisdom and oratorical powers as Jesus was must be a great prophet of God.

Jesus recognized him almost at once in the crowd and waved a welcome to him, "Simon, come nearer! I hoped you would come in search of Me. I have missed you. Rest here on this bench while I finish with the question just presented to Me."

It was dark by the time Jesus and Simon, arm in arm, reached the beach once more. The driftwood fires were lighted and the men huddled about them for the night was cold. To a man, they greeted Jesus enthusiastically.

This time the Nazarene's sermon treated of obedience to the Messiah. "Each individual soul," He said, "must rise to a state of interior peace above the anxious bodily interests of intemperance, lust, impatience, and avarice. Self-sacrifice and self-restraint are easy when God's love is the motive which absorbs a soul for its eternal gain."

As Jesus talked, Rosa-Maria made her way quietly through the darkness to a position just beyond the crowd of holy listeners. There she knelt, in the shadows, listening intensely to the Nazarene's voice which blended with the hum of the inky black waves that splashed near her feet. She believed what He said, and she instantly loved His voice and His calm kindness. But above all these virtues, she loved the assurance He gave her soul, the assurance not to fear God but to love Him. As she listened, she understood why Simon was willing to sell all of his possessions and leave her alone. She, too, would like to leave all cares and go in search of the living Messiah.

At last the sermon was over, and as Simon walked slowly home he was joined by Rosa. Both were filled with gladness and peace; both felt the new birth of God's love within their souls.

As they entered their home they saw Andrew on his knees caught up in the deepest prayer of quiet. Silently they knelt beside him. Andrew prayed for wisdom in regard to John's teaching, while Simon prayed for the grace with which to find the Messiah. Rosa prayed for the intentions of both men and for the hidden desires which they kept from each other. Was it possible, she asked herself, as she looked from one to the other, that both could be right?

*Excerpt from* The Refugee from Heaven—
*Book Five, Chapter Five: Peter's Enthronement*
Near the gate to the garden of Gethsemane lay an old log upon which Jesus, Peter, James, and John rested for a time before going on. Jesus said, "Peter, remove My sandals."

Peter was startled. His expression was one of grave question as he turned to his friends but they did not offer him any help or word. Kneeling at Jesus' feet, the big fisherman looked up at Him and said, "Jesus, I am not worthy to remove Your sandals. Only this minute I was remembering Your prediction that before dawn I would deny You. How then can I be worthy enough to perform this action? Lord, I am not worthy even to touch your sandals because I believe Your words. You are Truth—You are God. Lord and Master, save me from denying You before the cock crows at dawn. I cannot bear the thought. Please Jesus, give James or John the singular privilege of carrying out Your request."

Jesus moved His foot forward, kindly and gently and without another word, Peter quickly removed His sandal. At this moment of tremendous crisis of obedience, James and John walked on quietly toward the gate for they believed Jesus wanted to speak alone to Peter. The expression on Peter's face reminded them of the way he had looked caught up into the sleep of ecstasy when first he took the Living Bread into his hands.

Peter held the Master's sandal to his heart and bent forward in a mental prayer of gratitude and humility. Jesus said, "Peter, I have said that you will deny Me three times before the cock crows at dawn. Come, sit beside Me, while I tell you why I am allowing you, a victim of My will, to suffer the agony of such humiliation which will cause you to be chided, scolded, and ridiculed in the presence of friends until the end of time. There will be few people in time who will understand the true providence of God and His strategy in His war for souls and how I will use you and your successors, to the ends of endurance, as justifiers for Justice. This is both possible and reasonable when you understand that with Me there is no time and all is as present. I must take you into that realm of understanding and embarrass you for the need of great merit, through mortification, to you, yourself.

"Also, few people on earth will understand the deeper truths of My will because they will fail to believe that as long as time exists, human life will consist of warfare, on an actual battlefield, between the phenomenons of good and evil on earth. Every soul must be a soldier who is either for Me or against Me. That is why there is life and a battlefield.

"Because of all this, Peter, I have chosen you to be captain of My great army on earth. The effects of your mortifications, resulting into merit and grace, will be felt among your successors until the end of time.

"It will be the duty of such successors, or captains, to plan defensive maneuvers, not only for the day, but for the centuries to come. I have chosen you to suffer this great humiliation of denying Me because I have great need of the merit you will thus earn for the successors of My Church, which must be built on the foundation of humility. Peter, because you are hidden for a moment in the depths and truths of My will, I want you to know that mother and I have also exchanged hearts in this same fountain of union of wills together. Now that you and I have passed through that channel of greater love and perpetual understanding, you, too, will act for Me while you live on earth.

"In this the night of your soul, or agony, known as partial suspension of will hidden in the delights of My love, I am allowing you to understand—for this hour only—the plan of the great work I have prepared for you to accomplish. You see, I trust you will accept this humiliation, just as a soldier accepts a command to go alone into the night in order to save people whom he will never know, nor see, in life. A true soldier does not question why he is chosen—he simply obeys, even if it costs him his life, for hasn't a soldier given his will to conform to that of a superior for the greater good?

"Peter, your memory, according to earthly way of thinking and reasoning, will cease to recall our present words and plans after this hour of great ecstasy. The state of ecstasy has a way of deadening the human senses for a time according to quick reasoning, just as schooling teaches the mind. Our language consists of no words, but only the striking of My will upon soul and spirit, and one's actions and words are often motivated by habit according to the place and time and how he is questioned.

"After the denial tomorrow you will recall this hour slowly as if it were a dream when your mind is refreshed in the finite way of life, but you must keep your thoughts and My plans to yourself. Before you deny Me, and at a time when you will least expect it, I will withdraw special graces of loyalty from you. In your own human weakness, because you will try to save yourself from My enemies, you will deny Me in a moment of soul-weakness which is governed by fear in its pursuit of security.

*It is necessary for you to be clothed in the cloak of humility,*
*for in humility, on humility, and through humility*
*there is safety in the world for you and your successors.*

"Later, in the finite expression of awakening to reality, your spirit will feel the greatest inner pain of remorse, because you have now, at this hour, tasted of ethereal knowledge through ecstasy. I will allow the whip of remorse to strike your spirit as though it were a scourge as a means of meriting humility for you and your successors. I also want another kind of merit which comes from silence. Keep silent on these matters when you are accused, rather than try to excuse yourself or explain our plan for your successors. I will allow all these plans to be made known when I will.

"Peter, you will gain great merit in your silence and tears, and a furrowed brow will be your earthly crown. Spiritual nights will take hold of you, and you will at times think all is delusion, and the knowledge of My interior voice error. It is necessary for you to be clothed in the cloak of humility, for in humility, on humility, and through humility there is safety in the world for you and your successors. This ecstatic gift of intuitive knowledge is great and unique, and will not be enjoyed by many of your successors. There will be great captains in the last ages to come, and you will help them because of your penances and mortifications and willingness to follow My plan in the world-wide war for souls."

Jesus smiled and continued. "Since you have removed My sandal, Peter, it pleases Me to tell you that your gesture of holding it in your hand is your actual enthronement, as such exterior manifestations are allowed in our poverty. Most of your successors will be enthroned in the ceremonial splendors of their day. They will wear elaborate robes and gowns and colors for all occasions, but these poor, worn sandals, Peter, are all I have to offer you on this, your day, to assume your kingship on earth."

Peter's spirit was still wrapped in the delights of ecstasy. Kneeling before Jesus, he found himself watching the illustrious light and splendor of Heaven's gifts through which he was permitted to see, as well as understand, this sublime moment of his enthronement. Untold numbers of heaven's angels watched and honored him with unequaled grandeur of celebration and pomp and assembled at the Master's feet to await his coronation. With the shimmering light from their crowns of celestial light and power they followed, as with prophetic interest, all the coming ages and the splendor of his successors' enthronements. He saw each one with his vices and his sins— nothing was hidden from the celestial vision given him, for all is seen in the mind of God. And seeing certain pontiffs upon whom he gazed, he looked at Jesus and said smiling, "I will gladly follow Your will. Give me all the humiliations You wish."

Turning again to the vision's light of knowledge, he smiled as he watched the angels attend each of his successors and was enthralled as he saw most of them sing praises to his name for his sorrows and willingness to suffer all manner of ridicule until the end of time for having denied Jesus in, and through, the plan of Providence.

Peter awakened from his divine slumber of ecstasy and exclaimed aloud in awed wonderment, "Jesus, permit my name and my faults, especially my fault of denying You, to be discussed throughout the ages to come. I understand it is all for the greater good. Humble me, Lord, at every moment of time. And while I live, allow me the privilege of becoming a lesson of tears and silence in order to prove my love for You and my charity to Your friends. Jesus, my will is Yours for all time—do with me as You will. I could only will never to die in order to suffer this humiliation every minute of time. Well I understand, in the wisdom You have taught me, that there is really no time according to the understanding of ethereal knowledge. Therefore to spend a life-time in order to win souls, even through the gift of tears and humilia-tion, I know would, and could be, the greatest joy on earth."

As Peter's colloquy of holy desire ended, and he was once more free in the exterior world of thought, he removed the Master's other sandal without being bid to do so. Jesus arose barefoot and motioned Peter to be seated in His place. Then the Master knelt before him and re-moved his sandals quickly, replacing them with His own. As Jesus tied the laces, tears coursed down Peter's face for he realized humbly the wonderful significancè and profound meaning of being dressed in the clothes of the Master. He was the first Vicar of Jesus Christ on earth.

Still kneeling, Jesus clasped His hands in prayer and bowing His head in Peter's lap, said quietly, "Most Holy Father on earth, I humble Myself as your subject. I beg your permission to enter the garden with James and John to pray. And I beg you, Holy Father, to accompany us. We desire your holy friendship."

Peter was awestruck at such self-abjection, reverence to authority, and humility Jesus was showering upon him. He could not answer. He could only gasp for breath. This was indeed a shock of greater depth than his wearing the Master's sandals. He didn't realize that from that instant Jesus was his prisoner. He, Peter, was the prison-keeper and the keeper of the keys!

Then, remembering the Master's reason for his enthronement, obeying and honoring the privilege given him, he raised his hand in blessing over Jesus, and setting an example for all future priests and successors, exercised his authority which gave his spirit and body a foretaste of martyrdom, by granting God—this Jesus on earth—per-mission to pray in the garden. He reasoned to himself that Jesus was giving him a lesson on how men should follow Him by first asking permission from one in authority before attempting any work on earth according to one's own will and pleasure. Indeed the Master humbles Himself to His servants! In that moment of asking Peter's permis-sion, Jesus as true Man had willingly, and for a moment, forgotten

His divinity, better that He might shoulder the burden of true Man, by humbly asking permission from one in authority. Christ is the way! As true Man He was preparing Himself for the agony by this humble submission of asking permission.

Peter answered, "Jesus, Son of God, You have my permission to enter into the garden with James and John. I will go with You."

Jesus kissed Peter's hand, turned, and going to where James and John waited, walked with them through the gates of Gethsemane. Peter, carrying his own sandals in his hand, followed the little procession in stunned wonderment. He tried to walk in each footprint made by the bare feet of the Master as He led them through the narrow paths to the interior garden.

*End of Excerpts from* The Refuge From Heaven

*Excerpt from the* Letter Lessons
Note: The *Letter Lessons* are weekly meditations and actions to be taken by the participant in this thirty-one week spiritual journey. Each letter (addressed to Father Frank Parrish, S.J.) recommends Scripture study and disciplines (mortification of the senses), exercises in humility designed to bring one to a better understanding of daily living with the indwelling presence of Christ, and the active role of contemplative prayer.

*A.M.D.G.*[32]
*First Letter Lesson*
*January 11, 1954*
*Dear Father,*
I am writing this in answer to your request that I write the mystical steps of knowledge given to me by Saint Aloysius.[33] I must admit that your request leaves me with a feeling of utter helplessness, but with God's guiding grace, I hope to accomplish the good you intend from this dark well of my memory. To begin such a task is only to lose

---

32 AMDG stands for the Latin motto of the Society of Jesus (Jesuits): *ad majorem Dei Gloriam* (for the greater glory of God)

33 There is a precedent in Catholic Church history regarding the appearance of saints. One well known example took place in 1633, when *Saint Francis Xavier* appeared multiple times to a Jesuit priest, *Father Mastrilli, S.J.,* and urged him to devote himself to the missions. The Novena of Grace traces its source to this apparition.

myself in the mystery of time and pretend that I am a citizen of Jerusalem taking notes from the Master's lips. I am just the reporter and of myself filled with many imperfections. The human mind and memories may be likened in symbol to a picture of a Christmas tree covered with glittering tinsel, rain, and years' collections of beautiful balls. In symbolic terms, these images may be understood as the winding tinsel being the path to perfection, the rain being the monotonies in life, and the bobbing spheres, the rise and fall of our mirrored souls. One day we are gold, another green, sometimes red with circles of gold, and here and there among the boughs, we find a day represented by a purple ball, and we must not forget the silver and the blue balls, now so beautiful in retrospect.

In the measurement of time in the eyes of God, we are as useless as the path of tinsel and as fragile as a tree ball. A tree is not trimmed for the sake of the tree. Man is not trimmed nor disciplined in body and soul by the monotonies of life for the sake of self. He is brought into perfection and beauty for the greater glory of God and that beauty and light might become one with God.

The period of time in which Saint Aloysius taught me was two years. In the artistry of his teachings, it must be remembered that he set up rules as daily guides, which were intended as daily reminders—as the SCALE [author's emphasis] of practice. He must smile as I write, for am I not a foreign correspondent? Ecstasy language is not heard—the natural ear at that time is dead—can a dead ear hear? And so it is that I translate a language that is not a language—it is a mere tuning of His will upon my spirit—His divine impulses playing upon me as if I were a violin.

Jesus invited us all to "follow" Him. He is the Master of all perfection. Then it is only reasonable that He wants us to become masters of self. Let us pretend to pick ourselves up as if we were violins—instruments of tone. The five senses must learn to play upon the body and bring Heaven's grace down from Heaven. That grace, spiritual rain, waters the soul, and in turn the soul gives greater life to the spirit and the path or ladder rungs are formed and we begin the climb with our cross to God. The spirit leads, the soul follows, and the five senses follow as train-bearers for a bride. Every good done in life is a mystical procession of ourselves, a family, before Heaven's courts.

The word "meditation" is a medium word of power and meaning. It is a heritage of good earth in which the roots must be planted for our spiritual growth in the climb of contemplation. Meditation is usually the formation of simple lip service fostered by the atmosphere of soul and its longing to visit with spirit. That union of perfect oneness, even before death, is known as "contemplation" and that word is learned, loved, and known when it is understood as "application."

Saint James caught the spirit of the Master's teachings in His words, "Be doers of the word"—doers of the lip service which gives us the title of "Samaritans" (see James 1:22–27). With our lips we have said in meditation prayer that we love—now in contemplation we must love, and that is zeal. Public prayers are seeds sown in the earth (our bodies), but contemplation is the planter, the worker, the tireless plougher and giver to the earth, for seldom is a harvest kept by the farmer. He shares his best fruits with his friends and the poor in spirit. And as the rain falls upon our parched earth, it is the divine impulses of the Son after His glorious Resurrection. The mountain streams for our fields are our own tears of either joys or sorrows. With our house (body) set in order, we should each become pillars and fires for God while we sojourn on earth (see Lk 12:49–50).

There is a time and a place for everything in life, and application to every hour—even in the hours of sleep. Are we not then the imitators in the tomb? And friends should be selected as carefully as we would select jewels for a queen's crown from a jeweler's collection (see Prv 22:24–25 and Eccl 6). If, at any time, a person may prove to lead us farther away from God, then it is better that we close the book of his or her life in our lives with the sureness that we would close a useless book on the shelf of a library. We must be gracious though in that library and place not dust upon the book, for the book could be a guide, a bookmark for a meditation student.

Charity begins at home. That home referred to in Scripture is our own individual body. We must not lose sight of the truth that we are God's tabernacles as surely as if we were on wheels imitating the ark of the covenant. We must not adorn that tabernacle with crosses God did not intend for us to have by being busybodies about neighbors' business through which we could pick up a cross. Every shoulder is formed for a certain cross, which God will give or allow, but it is not fashioned for crosses of the neighbors. We must stay simple and not burdened with many cares, and [eliminate] the cares that cross our minds if they do not belong to our state in life or vocation. We shall then balance the inventory by erasing the unnecessary cares in life.

Father, about the time Saint Aloysius taught me the easy steps for a convert child, I heard the Master say, "Calmness of mind shall be greatly rewarded." Then our saint taught me that calmness is the ability to think carefully and weigh well the subject matter in the balance of justice. It is quite necessary for our formal reading to acquaint us with Scripture, both the Old and the New Testaments. Also, history should be a part of our diets. These studies are the firm foundations for future contemplation. Contemplation is another form of invisible bilocation into the past where we may live with Christ and follow Him and become apprentices. An apprentice is an apprentice that he might become a master. Contemplation is to be alone with Jesus. Contemplatives do not mystically travel in groups. Oneness with God is all that matters in the Oneness of God.

It is during visitation with friends and group enjoyments that we should trade our gifts as the Master commanded. Exchange of views is the stimulation good for the soul. In joy, spirit climbs in its mastery of love when fanned by the understanding of soul who like a mother disciplines the five senses as if they were tiny children playfully living within the tabernacle, the body.

Calmness is mastered greatly by the gift of *knowing* and *loving* silence (see Is 30:15). Silence has a great wardrobe, and daily we may wear new togas. We must watch carefully that we do not walk in muddy paths—arm in arm with evil friends. Dry cleaning for togas and especially for the rising master is most difficult and expensive. Dry cleaning is the confessional cleaning. To speak of faults and the soil of life is only to let the good confessor know our heights and delights— this is mortification to both body and senses.

*Application and Sense Mortification*
Application is zeal for the love of God. Simple applications for the week are: First, we shall walk daily around a city block and smile and greet even strangers with a cheery, "Good morning" and smile. Three souls must be greeted on the streets (a walk to the office, certain building,

or markets may take the place of the city block. The people should be strangers—not the usual gardener, grocer, or busman). Every day for a week a letter to a sick friend[34] or shut-in must be written. Jesus follows us everywhere;—an apprentice follows His "way." One day during the week we must seek Him in three different churches and make a visit without the usual formal prayers such as reading prayers. Our just talking to Him proves to Him that if we were living in Jerusalem we would be willing to "follow Him" for even three days without care of rest or food. Also, we must mortify the sense of sight five times a day (no more nor less). We must practice overcoming being a "detailist"— this is most important when talking with friends. Few words should be our goal. As we kneel alone three times each day and bow deeply before divine justice of God, we shall reverently kiss the floor each time as if we were kissing His garment. And finally, with the counter beads, we shall move up one bead each time we have broken silence willfully prying into the affairs of others; we shall move a bead if we revel in relating all the latest news without being asked (this could be a curb for idle words).

Our penance for each bead moved during the day must bring its punishment. Remembering Christ within is, and how He hated lack of zeal and said through the Spirit that He would "vomit" the luke-warm out of his mouth (Rev 3:16), [the penance] is for us to actually taste of lukewarm by drinking a cup of warm coffee or tea or milk for each bead moved. And forgetting the lukewarm penance until night or even until bedtime does not alter the matter—we must drink all the number of cups (without a scowl, always).

*Scripture Study*
During the day or better at bedtime we may begin the habit if we do not already have it, of Scripture reading by daily studying well these quotations of Saint Peter and the ones quoted [above] at least once during the week:

---

34 In his book, *The Unseen Power of Prayer* (Our Sunday Visitor Publishing), *Michael McDevitt* tells the story of the dramatic impact this exercise—writing a letter to a sick friend—had on his life and how it affirmed his spiritual connection with *Cora Evans*.

- 1 Pt 3:13–15, "And who is there to harm you, if you are zealous for what is good? But even if you suffer anything for Justice' sake, blessed are you. So have no fear of their fear and do not be troubled. But hallow the Lord Christ in your hearts" (the indwelling). "Be ready always with an answer to everyone who asks a reason for the hope that is in you" (the reason for more study).
- 1 Pt 4:1, "Since Christ therefore has suffered in the flesh, do you also arm yourselves with the same intent, because he who has suffered in the flesh has ceased from sin, that during the rest of his time in the flesh he may live no longer according to the lust of man, but according to the will of God." When suffering to the flesh comes from God, through the fall of Adam, and when mortifications become an application, we are arming ourselves with Christ and putting "off the old man" (see Col 3:5–11) of lustful earth for the Christ within us.

Let us develop into masters for the Master (see Lk 6:40). "Live in peace . . . the God of love and of peace shall be with you" (see 2 Cor 13:11).

*Devotedly in the Sacred Heart of Jesus,*
Signed: Cora

*Tapestry (1950)*[35]
A pilgrim, the symbol of you and me, knelt on the sands of time. As she prayed in simple words of praise, her gaze bent heavenward, and there in Heaven's avenues of blue she watched a flowing scene of golden mists, reminding her of streams of incense smoke, all coming down her way. She wondered what the golden streamlets were and what they symbolized as the billowing cloud rose and fell as tide at her feet.

From out of the golden vapors an angel appeared, and he answered, "These are the harp strings from the Master's heart. They are expressions, or paths, of His love to you. In His love for you He is lending you

---

35 Publisher's note: Cora's daughter, *Dorothy Evans*, considered *Tapestry* to be most meaningful: "My greatest consolation in all this is the Master's love letter on the tapestry of life."

His light, the harp of His Heart. His Heart is a loom, little soul, and on that loom He wishes for you to weave the tapestry of your life. Make it beautiful, for someday He will walk on that tapestry of life when He comes to take you home.

"Now here at your side are three baskets of yarn, one black, one red, and one gold. These are the only colors necessary for the weaving of a tapestry, for they symbolize every mood and walk of life. Symbolized here in black are days of dismay, spiritual darkness, discouragement, and doubt. The red yarns symbolize days of pain, mental torture, conflicts between nations, and strife and poverty among friends. The golden threads are expressions of God's consolations, feast days, Holy Communions, and anniversary joys in every state of life. Now with these yarns, little soul, carefully weave the tapestry of your life. Make it beautiful, for nothing is too good for God.

"Do you know, little soul, God is a hobby collector, a collector of beautiful souls? Often when souls are asleep at night, He tiptoes to the earth's looms hidden in His Heart, and from those He quietly snips the tapestries of love from each loom. Then with His collection of joy, He hurries to His archives above where the angels and saints stand aghast, and breathlessly transfixed they whisper, 'What is He going to show us today, and who is He going to tell us about?'

"Little soul, if you could only see His joy, His smile, His hurried stride, you would weave your tapestry all for His love. With jubilant gestures, in the great halls above, He unfurls the tapestries of life for angels and saints to enjoy. All Heaven is hushed, then words of praise and joyful shouts fill the awesomeness of Heaven as all exclaim, 'Jesus, it is beautiful! And this one is majestic. Ah, this one is an illustrious symphonious poem, and look, not a knot on either side. Is it possible for a soul to live on earth without a thought of rebellion to authority, which this tapestry reveals in its intricate weave? Oh God, tell us to whom this one belongs.'

"Oh little soul, His smile was glorious as He answered, 'This tapestry belongs to Father Frank; he is a soldier in My Society on earth.' The angels and saints all knelt as they gazed upon the wonderment of his soul, and as they watched the pattern unfold, they exclaimed with awed expressions, 'Just look, a golden gauntlet lying on a background of black. Why, this is a symbol of the Master's hand of authority in a world of utter blackness! And look, a huge white-gold horse, the symbol of Christ's own horse as told in the book of the Apocalypse."

The courts of heaven sighed and marveled as the tapestry slowly unrolled to reveal to them the Warrior Christ on His horse, with His bow all set to strike the darkness where lay His gauntlet on the ground. A sigh of tones rose and fell over the fairways of Heaven with this exclamation, "Jesus, the Conqueror to conquer the souls of unlawful joys."

"Little soul, the Master's smile was glorious as He asked His courts of Heaven to watch with Him a phenomena of the tapestry. Suddenly, the face of Christ in the tapestry weave was the picture of Father Frank. Yes, Father Frank was astride that horse—he was earth's figure of another Christ set to conquer the piteous and perilous will of man. A joyous shout arose, and in the din of praise to Father Frank, the angels and saints asked, 'Jesus, tell us the theme of Father's song and thoughts as he weaves his tapestry of life.' Jesus, the hobby collector of beautiful souls, threw back His broad shoulders and sang aloud these words, 'O Heart of Jesus, the loom of my love, come down into my heart and lend me the chiming of time, for the timing of time is the chimes of Thy Heart. O Heart of Jesus, help me to weave on Thy loom the patterns of souls who have lost the shuttle of goodwill to delight Thee in the shadows of black, gold, and red.'"

"Oh little soul," continued the angel, "would you, through sin and selfishness, deny God that pleasure of displaying His hobby collection of beautiful souls? Remember, His delights are to be with the children of men, both in Heaven and on earth. We love to hear of them and they love to hear of us."

The angel disappeared. The little pilgrim, the symbol of you and me, slowly pushed aside the baskets of yarn in the colors of black and red, and mused aloud, "Why should I use the black and red? I'll use nothing but the gold, for nothing is too good for God."

All day she wove with the threads of gold. Little did she realize that when the sun took its rest in the west that the gold of her tapestry, too, would take its rest. And that it would appear lifeless and tarnished in the grey of the night. Little did she realize the reason for the color of black, for without blackness to give depth to the night we would never see the immensities of God in the universe. Without black we could not see the stars and the moon and feel the natural longing for death, for sleep is a form of death. Without the red in all earth's tapestries of life, our loss would be the glorious sunsets, painted clouds, and the golden rise of morning, which breathes of new life and hope in the resurrection.

The little pilgrim, the symbol of you and me, wept bitterly as she realized the sorrows of gloom in the tarnished threads of disobedience which she had woven in the loom of His Heart. Now, she realized it was necessary to weave with the colors of life—the black, the red, and the gold. Why, each color enhanced the other in outline and depth and gave life to the emblematical patterns of souls.

The angel was again at her side, and he spoke in a voice of grave concern, "I told you to weave with the yarns of black and the red and the gold. Why just look, your weaving with gold would tell me your life was all gold. You are finite; you cannot live without the colors of black and red. Tear it all out."

Quickly, the pilgrim tore the tarnished threads from the loom while her angel continued to scold, "Ah, such piteous self-love and self-will you have woven today. I trust you will learn to obey, for obedience is the Master's way to eternal life. Ask God to give you the grace to obey, lest you deny Him the joys of His Will to find joys with the children of men."

The tarnished yarns were removed, and the pilgrim, the symbol of you and me, fell to her knees and wept aloud these words, "I'm sorry, God. Help me to follow the pattern of life. Help me to weave a pattern of beauty for Thee with the black, the red, and the gold."

Her angel listened to her prayer, and then he answered, "Listen carefully now to what I'm going to say. Take your three baskets of yarn to the weaver of destinies, Thy priest, and tell him what you have. The priest knows the pattern to choose for you, for he knows the pattern of life, death, and resurrection. And he will lend you the protective shelter of his cloak, the priesthood, if you but ask for his care. The patterns he chooses for many are beautiful, while others are majestic, and many others are simple, but regardless of the design he chooses for you, little soul, weave that pattern carefully and without complaint. And notice when you give him the shuttle of your will, first he will wind the yarn of black, then gold, and then red."

*Golden Detachment in the Soul* Complete Text
*May 27, 1947*

As the last words were written on the writing titled, "Our Lord's Forty Days in the Desert,'" I knelt to thank Jesus for His gift of knowledge in writing which He had given me. I was glad to describe His life and infinite love toward our world with my finite expressions, and I gave Him all praise for those thoughts. Through the gift of the contemplative life, human words that heretofore seemed ugly and unrefined now appeared to my soul as brushes in the hands of an artist, willing and ready to go to work in His love.

As I continued to pray, I suddenly felt the wondrous nearness of Jesus Himself. There he stood before me in all the splendor of His divine Humanity. My soul, as a poor weak prisoner, felt the suffering of nothingness. Slowly, as if He silently commanded me, I gazed into His eyes. His returning gaze of understanding love gave me courage to remain kneeling in adoration before His real, unspeakable majesty. His voice of ravishing delight to all the senses pierced my soul with these words, "Do you realize the gift you have? Could you love Me more if I gave you more?"

My soul seemed to wither away at the thought of such a question. I tried to reason within myself for the answer in relation to God's Wisdom. While I remained in silent thought, I was suddenly transported in spirit into a moment of God's eternal light. There, a sudden illumination of knowledge bathed my soul in the deeper gifts of divine understanding. There, in those terrible and profound depths and in the hidden love of each gift of knowledge, I felt God's invisible and enkindling Wisdom, judgment, and love fall across my soul. I was most unworthy of such delightful gifts. I tried to remember I was but a poor, weak creature filled with suffering emotions because I had not walked the narrow path of perfection, with the higher grace of perfect resignation to my own will in little things. With the knowledge of such tremendous gifts flooding upon my soul and the knowledge of my unworthiness through the light of God, I remembered I could not answer His question whether or not I could love Him more if He gave me more gifts. To answer in any earthly word of praise or exclamation would be a hindrance in expression[36] to

---

36  Publisher's note: Cora seems to say that to try to put her response into mere words would keep her soul from expressing a more profound answer.

the soul that, silenced with its gaze of love, were the golden musings of wisdom in all His answers as my soul's eyes visioning the holiness of Jesus. In those moments of delightful musings, just looking into His holy eyes, I longed above everything else to remain childlike to Jesus and not to have any love for Him measured by supernatural gifts. Then memory reminded me my will was not my own. I had offered it to God through Father Frank. I had no right to make such decisions in the fields of grace. Father Frank was the lawmaker of my soul in the gifts of the spiritual life, and I must consult him about the question and the answer: Could I love Jesus more if He gave me more gifts?

Again our Lord's ravishing voice asked, "Do you realize the gift you have? This is the first time I have given to the world the details of My life. I am giving My friends this gift through you, better to establish My kingdom of love within souls. I desire all souls to know I am real, I am alive, and the same today as after the Resurrection. The greater knowledge of My kingdom in souls is but another step towards the Golden Age. Golden, because souls in sanctifying grace will resemble the light of the golden sun and in that golden kingdom, I may personally dwell if I am invited. For I have said, 'The kingdom of God is within you.' Through this knowledge many souls will loan me their bodies, and in this way they actually become My Mystical Humanity. My borrowed Humanity, My other Humanity, and in them I relive My life on earth as I did after the Resurrection, and in them I cause a beautiful transfiguration." I could not answer nor thank Jesus for His great gifts. All thoughts of gratitude seemed to freeze upon my lips and heart, and I knelt to kiss the floor where He stood. My soul cried out these words, "O crucible Love! O crucible Love! Keep me ever near Thy Heart! O crucible Love! Give me the memory of Thy voice. May Thy voice become my life, my death, and resurrection." From His gown near His Heart, Jesus removed a large golden lock. Its half-circle arm or lock-haft was closed into the main part of the lock. I noticed the lock was without a key. Graciously Jesus handed me the lock, and as He did so He spoke these words, "Here ask Father." The vision ended. As I recollected myself I could not understand just what I should ask Father. However, I resolved to tell him the complete vision and to follow his advice.

Later, when I had talked with Father, and after much thought, he advised me to allow God to have His way in my soul and to accept any gift the Master desired to give me. Also, I must trust that Jesus would protect me against pride and offer all the gifts, especially the one of writing, as an act of a continuous praise for the glory of God. And I was to remember, after having asked Father's guidance and permission to receive God's graces, that I would be doubly protected from the attacks of the evil [one] in his quest to discourage my soul in the love of God. Father asked me to write the knowledge of the vision and the words of Jesus. Now, once again, I threw myself into the mercy of the Holy Spirit, and with this prayer I cried, "O Holy Spirit, hold me to Thy light! Protect and govern me in understanding and will. Teach me language of the celestial essence for the earth, for I have seen many things without seeing. I have heard many things without hearing: many gifts which I have seen were understood and loved to the soul alone and they were expression, yet I must write about them because Father has willed so. O Holy Spirit, I cling to Thy gown of fortitude, joy, and mercy. O Holy Spirit, I know You understand how I long for solitude and quietness of the inner self. Oh, it is truly a world with expressions, but without words. That world I long for. O Holy Spirit, guide my hand in writing for the continuous praise of God. Help me in the celestial language to write it through the door of God for those of this world."

The next evening my soul was caught up into a divine slumber after the same manner and expression of love as I had experienced in the year of 1945, and again I felt myself as a tiny infant in the holy arms of Jesus as He skated over the ice of my heart—the symbol of my detachment from the things of the world. The ice was not gray and cold-looking as it was in 1945, but it glowed in numberless rising mists of gold.

As we walked on, a narrow, golden path circled before us, leading away from the main sea of golden ice. It circled out into the eternal silence and seizing darkness as a bridge of gold. Then I understood the narrow path was the haft of the golden lock which Jesus had handed to me the day before, when He asked me to ask Father if I should receive more graces and more gifts. The golden lock was the symbol of my heart.

As we began to walk on the narrow pathway, Jesus spoke, "We are walking upon the lock, the symbol of your heart. Your soul is the lock of many locks to My Heart. The knowledge that you have received has been your unlocking of MY Heart through perfect trusting I would give you anything for the use of MY glory. From this minute, you hold the key of My Heart through the wisdom of trust. You may unlock My treasures at will through the governing powers of Father. Other souls, too, may become keys to this way of love by walking upon this path of perfection that we are now on after they have turned a deaf ear to the calling of the world and its forbidden pleasures. All gifts are forbidden if they forget Me as their constant Companion. Have no gift that you cannot share with Me.

"Detachment is for this. The narrow path to My Heart must be put to a test—not for a day or a week—perhaps for several years. This way of perfection may be gained by all vocations in life. The fruits of the narrow path are simple, childlike prayer—just talking to Me in My Humanity through the gates of the Blessed Sacrament.

"Incredible calmness is next—calmness to the extent that life becomes a joyous thought of willingness to please Me above everything else, in sorrows and in joys.

"Selflessness is next. Do for others before considering thy own self even in little pleasures of the world. Always deny thyself so that others might have."

As we neared the center of the circling half of the lock, or the narrow path of gold, we stopped to gaze into the dark depths of eternal nothingness. It resembled a dark circular sea that lay between the main lock and the circling half, and Jesus asked, "Do you see anything in the mirrored darkness?"

I answered, "No."

Jesus continued, "If you should be so unfortunate as to leave this narrow path, I may have to bring you here from time to time to show you the attachment on earth that you have placed above the thought of Me. I assure you, to vision [view] any love above the love of Me in this darkness would be painful to both soul and body. It would be equal to the depth of purgatorial suffering."

My soul shuddered at His words, and silently I prayed for the grace to never fail my Jesus. For I feared above everything else to be walking along the side of Jesus and have my sins mirrored before me rather than see His smiling face.

As we walked along toward the main part of the lock, Jesus spoke again in a most beautiful and humorous way, "This is a very narrow path. It is only wide enough for two, just you and Me. When you could not answer Me as to whether you could love Me more if I gave you more gifts, all that was the effect of obedience on your soul, for you speak only through Father."

Then with a smile He continued, "I could almost become jealous over your solicitude and obedience to Father above Me. Nothing pleases Me more than this way of obedience—your will through the will of my priests. Souls are privileged to follow this way of obedience, for only through My priests' guidance can souls walk upon the gold of their heart in its way of purgation while they live on earth. There is no other way to the higher way of perfection. My priests are the only ones who can open the door."

As we walked on in silence, I realized that I must walk alone now into the depths of the lock. I understood my body and soul represented the secret key. It would unlock the lock and thus release the haft, and I wondered and shuddered. Would this be the moment of my death on earth? Would this be the living death Saint Paul spoke about? "I die daily" [1 Cor 15:31]. Or, would this be a living death from time to time, such as divine slumber, the better for me to lift from His hidden treasures the knowledge and hidden meaning in Christ's life on earth? The questions raced through my mind as I descended into the lock. There as I slowly descended and as I took each step, I felt the radiance of unequaled grandeur of light revolving about me and coming up from inside the lock. Light, like revolving rainbow arches, one after another as far as the spiritual eye could see, rolling toward me. There in those arches of unexplainable glory stood thousands of angels, all in human form. They were adoring God in an act of deep reverence. As I watched them, I seemed to fall into a rapture of dreadful pain—pain to both body and soul at once—a type of pain that I had never experienced, yet it was beautiful and pleasing to the soul and terrifying in excessive exhaustion to the human body. I did not plead for mercy, for I seemed to understand it was a pain of purgation—a purgation necessary to have in order to be near the angels of such holiness.

Suddenly all the angels turned toward me. From their eyes seemed to flow great, narrow streams of living fire and all directed at my heart. As each flame left its burning delight upon my heart, I felt the joy of desiring to love Jesus more and more. As the vision ended, and

I left the vastness of the interior lock, I heard my soul addressing the Holy Spirit in these words, "O Holy Spirit, don't ever leave me. Take my hand and lead me on the narrow path. There instill in all my senses the holy knowledge that I must love God more and more. Blind my eyes, O Holy Spirit, if by chance I may love some other object more than God. Never, never, O Holy Spirit, let me fall. Never let me see the world's gifts I would choose above Christ's holy face. Never, never, O Holy Spirit, let me fall. But help me, O Holy Spirit, to fall in adoration before my Jesus."

*In a letter to her spiritual director, Father Frank,*
*Cora wrote about the Sacred Heart of Jesus.*
*The entire letter is included on the following pages.*
*A.M.D.G.*
*Dear Father,*

A convert's mind is often filled with astonishment and gratitude as mystery after mystery is unveiled, such as the Sacred Heart revelation—all is beyond our word expression. Since you have asked me to write you a few thoughts on how I accepted the Sacred Heart devotions and how the mysteries struck upon my mind, I will in turn ask you mystically to kneel before the shrine of His Heart where I knelt eighteen years ago. There, I will try in some measure to portray to you some of my most interior thoughts, analysis, and vision on how each untangled truth formed an invisible indestructible chain around my entire life.

First, I allowed my mind to skip back through the ages of which history had taught me, and there I envisioned myself watching the caravan of people led by Moses through the desert. The mystery was slowly traveling with them for forty years. The vastness of the desert was overwhelming! The heat was unbearable. Water was rationed. Children suffered and died, and parents murmured about the judgment of Moses to have taken them from the valley where water was plentiful. They reasoned their condition then was better than the present, even though they had been in bondage.

Their murmurings forced Moses into great depths of prayer. And God heard his lamentations and gave the earth a visible, actual vision of Himself, the First Person, as a pillar of fire reaching from Heaven to the earth. Through knowledge study of Scripture, I knew the expression that *God walked and talked with Moses* was made possible by an angel in an assumed form, as man acting as an ambassador. But in this history-turning event for the future Christendom, God in His divine mercy Himself came down to the people as a pillar of fire. It is known that God, formless Spirit, appeared many times as fire during the history-making of Scripture.

Returning to our mind's vision, the great pillar of fire, reaching from Heaven to the earth, traveled ahead of the caravan. It was something for the people to gaze upon, wonder about, and a goal in life to reach through the revealing of mystery. It was also a truth made visible that there was a God and that Moses was a prophet. The pillar of fire was their light by night and their cloud-shadow from the terrible heat by day. Let us imagine the word *pillar* had not been invented and the word *river* had been used for that great beam of light. Let us consider it as Heaven's golden river giving gold, wealth, and mystery to those who will seek after it. It is reasonable to think that Moses and his people were having a foretaste of Heaven as they gazed upon that river of gold. The phrase "foretaste of Heaven" rang a bell in my mind, and instantly I shifted in time to the life of Christ.

Let us mingle with the crowds as they hovered around Him. He is saying, "The Father and I are ONE; he who hears Me hears the Father." What a startling truth! Just think, God the Spirit no longer needed an angel ambassador—this Jesus was the mediator between Heaven and earth!

What a truth to realize that the Human nature of Christ was the vase which held and hid from our sight the golden river, the Divinity! Come, we may draw closer to the golden river, and we may touch it if we touch Christ. What a singular privilege, above that which Moses and his followers had during their forty years.

The golden river was again upon the earth! Let us listen again to Jesus. He is [speaking] to the people around Him who believe in the mystery of the Incarnation and yet who fear that the world will never again see the pillar of fire, which had meant so much to them as a foundation of truth. Jesus is saying, "Friends, to a few on earth I will give a foretaste of Heaven as you have known the golden river." Let us consider the actual phrase in that sentence which reads, "To a few on earth I will give a foretaste of Heaven." What a promise! Let us imagine how the people cheered that their choicest delight had not been taken from the earth.

That promise is most astonishing—a promise given by the God-Man. How would He accomplish the mystery now that He was on earth? No doubt thousands of other people wondered how the mystery would be performed, and when it happened again on earth it would be one of the greatest proofs that Jesus was the God-Man.

Father, as I continued kneeling before the shrine, my mind's knowledge of history seemed to speak these thoughts, "The coming down of the Holy Spirit was an avalanche of His generosity. With His fan, He was actually scattering the pillar of fire over the earth. He turned the golden river into streamlets and allowed them to become absorbed into the apostles. And Jesus said, "I have come into the world to cast My fires out upon the world and what would I but that you become enkindled!"

Then I knew the sadness of misinterpretation. That fire does not mean earthly devastation or the destruction of the universe. It simply means the golden river since the coming down of the Holy Spirit would destroy the old potter's clay, the human, unguided senses known as the old man and refine them, through fire, into a new world—a new body which would be a fitting place for His indwelling. How wonderful to know the golden river in us will actually deify man if he will only cooperate with grace. How wonderful to understand the will of Jesus who wishes for us to become One with Him as He and the Father are One. Our first principle of grace is the freedom to sip from the great reservoirs of knowledge the apostles reserved for us through the continual golden river known as Christ's priests.

And what other truths of His thoughtfulness! He knew that time has a way of making events seem fantastic and mythical. Therefore, He would use other people down through the ages, and to them He would give a foretaste of Heaven—the pillar of fire made visible again on earth. In our own age, He has made this mystery relive through the gifts of Saint Margaret Mary. For her, during one of her many ecstasies, He drew back the cloak from the region of His Heart, which is the expression of the organ of love, and through the Heart He allowed her to see a ray of the golden river.

Great intuitive knowledge was given her, and out of them she worded the twelve promises that we know today. How wonderful to know that she was seeing the same pillar of fire Moses and his followers enjoyed. How wonderful to know that she actually saw the same fire that came down on the apostles! To Saint Margaret Mary He gave the foretaste of Heaven that we may not waiver in the belief of prophets, mystery, and their fulfillment.

Father, I consider the apparition known to us as the Sacred Heart as the greatest happening on earth since the coming down of the Holy Spirit upon the apostles. We of this time since Christ must believe His words, "No one goes to the Father except through Me."

Let us become other little golden rivers through the practice of the indwelling. Let us seek the hidden people in the world who know not Christ, especially those in heresy, and with the golden light within us let us believe that His light will melt away the darkness—there is a dawn for everyone. Let us take the knowledge of the golden beam-like river and pretend it is a golden nail splintering into the wood of ourselves. The splintering cross on Calvary revealed new mysteries. They are the tokens of His love.

*Devotedly,*
Cora
(Original letter signed by Cora Evans)

# 5

# Homilies by Father Frank Parrish, S.J.

*Introduction*

FATHER FRANK WAS RENOWNED for his leadership as the Los Angeles Archdiocesan Director of the League of the Sacred Heart and the Apostleship of Prayer. Perhaps he is best known in Catholic circles for his blessing of a terminally ill priest, Father John Houle, S.J., with the relic of Blessed Claude de la Colombiere on February 23, 1990. This led to a miraculous cure: a first-class miracle, the miracle needed for the final step in the sainthood process. Claude was canonized by Pope John Paul II on May 31, 1992.

When we consider that Saint Claude, a Jesuit priest, was the spiritual director for a mystic, Saint Margaret Mary Alacoque, we believe it is no coincidence that the miracle was at the hands of a Jesuit priest who was the spiritual director for another mystic: Cora Evans. The connection is apparent when we consider the role of Saint Margaret Mary introducing the devotion to the Sacred Heart of Jesus, and Father Frank's leadership in promoting the devotion throughout Southern California.

We are fortunate to have hundreds of his homilies that were broadcast on the weekly *Catholic Quarter Hour*. The nine homilies selected here are taken from his book *Sparks from His Heart*.

*The Sacred Heart—Burning Furnace of Love*

No truer words were ever penned than those by the poet when he wrote, "It's love that makes the world go'round."

In the devotion to the Sacred Heart of Jesus, this driving power of love is lifted out of the quagmire of confusion and debasement as it is harmfully and wrongly thought of by so many today, and placed on the lofty spiritual and supernatural heights of God Himself.

Devotion to the Sacred Heart is not something out on the periphery of Catholic life. It is not a "fringe" devotion in the Church—a sort of an unnecessary accident, but it is at the core of our Faith—by the very fact that it deals with the mystery of our divine Savior's love. As a matter of fact, this devotion is most characteristic of Christianity because it is devotion to Jesus Christ Himself represented by the most essential organ of His Humanity, His Sacred Heart, which is the natural symbol of His love, both human and divine.

What is this love of which we speak? In answer I reply—it is the source of vital life to our Christian Faith. If the words of St. John—"God is love" (Jn 4:16) were not true, then none of us would have come into existence, nor would there be an everlasting dwelling place for us with Him in Heaven.

So when we say that it is love which makes the world go round, we might add here that without love none of us would have ever come into this world or been adopted as children of God, or be destined to enjoy eternal beatitude with Him. The love of our Savior, Jesus Christ, for each one of us, at Bethlehem, Nazareth, Jerusalem, and Calvary throughout His entire life, passion, and death is beautifully and most naturally symbolized by His Sacred Heart. In it is contained everything, for it speaks, not so much *WHAT* Christ has done for us, but *why* he did it—and this *why* is summarized in one word—love. Everything from the first moment of His conception to His dying gasp on the cross was dominated by the one impelling motive of love.

Today, how can we return our love to Christ for all He has done for us? The Apostleship of Prayer points out the way—by consecrating everything we do—our prayers, works, joys, and sufferings to the all-consuming interest burning in the Sacred Heart. This is a daily offering of our complete self—"a way of life"—a sort of living spirit of love, for love, behind all that we do.

In itself, the day which we offer up to our divine Lord to use for His purpose is of little account. But once He packs it full with His divine life and vitality, it becomes a means of returning our own personal love to him, and an instrument in the sanctification and salvation of others.

The Apostleship of Prayer also teaches us that this constant oneness with our Savior through His divine indwelling is made stronger and more vigorous by our being nourished on the Bread of Life through frequent Holy Communion and a deeper and more ardent love and devotion towards His Mother Mary. There was no one who was more conscious of His divine indwelling than was this woman, the master-piece of all His creations.

So, if you are looking for peace of mind in a world of confusion and have a burning desire to be one with Jesus Christ here on earth and for all eternity in Heaven, listen to these words of Pope Pius XII, who calls devotion to the Sacred Heart of Jesus "the highest act of religion."

Is there a devotion more excellent than that to the Most Sacred Heart of Jesus, one which is more in accord with the real nature of the Catholic Faith or which better meets the needs of the Church and the human race today? What act of religion is nobler, more suitable, sweeter, and more conducive to salvation, since this devotion is wholly directed to the love of God Himself?

So if you want to be loved—and we all do—you will find love in all its fullness in the Sacred Heart of Jesus. Your peace, joy, and happiness will be found within the shelter of His loving Heart.

And if you are moved by a lively sense of apostolic action, aflame with the desire of "the Sacred Heart for the world—the world for the Sacred Heart," listen to these words of the Holy Father. "It is also our most ardent desire that all who glory in the name of Christian and who zealously strive to establish the kingdom of Christ on earth, consider devotion to the Sacred Heart of Jesus as the standard and the source of unity, salvation, and peace."

No matter what your walk of life, no matter whether you are old or young, weak or strong, no matter where you live or work or play, you cannot escape the love burning in the Sacred Heart of Jesus. As in past centuries, when that same love fired the hearts of the apostles, confessors, martyrs, and virgins to acts of self-annihilation and heroic courage, so today divine love keeps that same flame leaping forth in all directions to strengthen and warm the hearts of our present-day apostles and teachers of the Word of God—yes, and our own martyrs and confessors, to live and even die for the love of their Eternal King and Savior, Jesus Christ.

God Bless and keep you in His Sacred Heart now and forever.

*Just Fifteen Seconds a Day*
Did you know that fifteen seconds can change your entire day? You struggle out of bed in the morning and face another eight-hour grind at the office or a monotonous day at the factory. You scramble off to school for another unexciting five hours of grueling exams and lectures. You see nothing glamorous in a washing machine full of soiled diapers or a sink full of dirty dishes. You find the joy of a smiling, friendly face so short-lived; the dull hammering pain of a headache—oh, so long lasting!! But, there can be something behind every action and duty, no matter how trivial or boring, that can transform it into something noble and eternally important. Yes, there can be something purposeful in the washer full of diapers—something meaningful in both the joys and sorrows, pains and aches, successes and failures of each day.

The difference in your day is the fifteen seconds it takes you to say, "The Morning Offering" prayer. With that daily offering as the purifying element of intention, every prayer, work, joy, and suffering of the day becomes fuel for that blazing furnace of divine love—the Sacred Heart of Jesus! Then your sink is linked to thousands of altars throughout the world; your headache is united with the slow, rotting martyrdom of an imprisoned priest in a concentration camp in China, your joys and successes rise up with the alleluias and hosannas to the Risen Savior; your whole life becomes a continued refrain of adoration, thanksgiving, praise and reparation to the Creator of the Universe—all for one fifteen-second "Morning Offering" of your day for the same intentions that burn in the Sacred Heart. This daily consecration of self through the Morning Offering prayer is the very essence of the Apostleship of Prayer, and because of it everything is transformed into supernatural value for all eternity. This is not a devotion, but a complete way of life. Through it, all people of every race and color, lay people, as well as those in the service of God, participate as hidden dynamos of supernatural power, thus not only sanctifying themselves but overflowing out to those who are near and dear—even to the farthest corners of the world!

Back in the year 1844, at Val, France, a Jesuit priest, Father Francis Xavier Gautrelet, realized the hidden value of this Apostleship of Prayer and inspired the young seminarians preparing for the priesthood and missionary life to be apostles at home, at least in spirit, while still in studies. He suggested that they daily offer up to God their prayers, duties, studies, play, and sacrifices, and through these to beg God's help for the priests and missionaries already in the field and the graces for conversions.

The suggestion caught fire and soon spread to neighboring villages, churches, convents, and other institutions. It wasn't long until the whole country of France and other countries were captivated by this idea of becoming apostles of prayer by this daily consecration of prayers, works, joys, and sufferings. Since then, the Apostleship of Prayer has spread throughout the world until today it is estimated that there are nearly forty million members, including six million in the United States alone. With it grew also the practice of First Friday Holy Communions of Reparation, the devotion of the Holy Hour, the Consecration of the Family, and other devotions to the Sacred Heart.

The tremendous success and secret of this crusade for souls is the fact that in it, we are all one in the Mystical Body of which Christ is the Head, and whatever good we do has an effect on the other members. I might liken this spread of sanctity to the chain reaction of a single atom splitting up, and then having an effect on another atom as it in turn splits up, and then another and another, millions of times over, each affecting the other until finally there is a mighty explosion. In the Mystical Body the impact of the total sanctity of each member is so supernaturally dynamic as to cover the whole face of the earth with the love of God. This is how we become twenty-four-hour-a-day apostles without going to the missions, without preaching sermons. This is the Apostleship of Prayer.

God Bless and keep you in His Sacred Heart now and forever.

*Mary Is My Mother*
Mary is my Mother!

One thought like this can do a great deal to foster a deep abiding love and devotion toward our Blessed Mother—a thought that can unite us as close as the bond between mother and child. Mary is my Mother! Why?

I call Mary my Mother because I know that through the infinite merits of her Son I have been raised up to a participation in His divine nature. I am reliving the life of Jesus Christ through the life of grace.

Truly then Mary is my Mother, because she beholds her Child in me. I know that by striving habitually for an awareness of the divine indwelling of Jesus Christ in me, I have a sure means of having Mary watch over and protect me as a loving mother. She cannot help but love me because I am her child. Every fiber of her humanity pours out in love for me because of this bond uniting us two together by the ties of sanctifying grace.

What a happy doctrine, to know that the Mother of God is also our mother, to know that we can be conscious of the fact that she feels toward us as any mother would toward her child. She is far more than a mother in a figurative sense. Mary is not merely *like* a mother; she is really our Mother!

Is not a mother one who gives life? And has not Mary given us life—no, not our physical, natural life, but far more important, the infinite, supernatural life of God in our souls—a life which here on earth is already a beginning of the glorious life we shall have in Heaven if we persevere in reliving the life of her Son through grace.

At an awesome moment in history, according to God's plan of redemption, it depended on Mary, on her free consent, whether or not this supernatural life would be imparted to us through our Lord Jesus Christ. By her free consent we were reborn to this divine life—raised up to the infinite plane of God Himself. So all-compelling was this tremendous gift that later on in the life of Saint Paul, he could cry out in rapture, "I live, now, not I but Christ lives in me" (Gal 2:20).

True, we are not God, but we have His life in us! We are not God, but we are God's own adopted children! We are not God, but we have the supernatural life of His only begotten Son dwelling in us! What a transforming gift! No wonder Saint John cried out: "And this is the testimony that God has given us, eternal life. And this life is in His Son. He that hath the Son hath life; He that hath not the Son hath not life. These things I write to you that you may know that you have eternal life, you who believe in the name of the Son of God" (1 Jn 5:11–13).

Mary is our Mother, because she has begotten us to this supernatural life of grace. In other words, it is to her, after Jesus Christ, that we are indebted for our supernatural life, this life of the children of God, and for whatever has to do with the production in us of that life, its preservation and development. She is our Mother, as it were, according to the spirit and in the order of grace because she is the Mother of our divine Savior according to the flesh and in the order of nature. It is to this great fact that the Fathers and Doctors of the Church constantly refer us as to the basis on which rests the spiritual motherhood of Mary.

The Mother of God is *our* Mother because she gave her free consent to the mystery of the Incarnation, for the Incarnation looked ahead to the passion and death of Him Who would be born of her as the condition of *our* rebirth. The Son of God became man that we might have His life through His death. That is why in God's divine Providence, Mary's consent was needed and why God left it to her free consent to accept a dignity involving so great a sacrifice. From the moment Mary declared to the Angel Gabriel that she accepted her maker's will— "Behold the Handmaid of the Lord, be it done unto me according to Thy Word (Lk 1:38), our redemption—our rebirth to the supernatural life—was assured. It was from that moment that we must date her spiritual motherhood in our regard.

We might add further that there is still something lacking to make that motherhood toward us complete. She must stand by the cross of Jesus and bring forth her spiritual children in anguish and bitterness of soul. As the Mother of all the living, she must give them spiritual life through the pangs of childbirth as she endures the passion of her Son. It was on Golgotha that Jesus won for us the grace of divine adoption by the outpouring of His Blood. How very much in order it was, then, that He should crown His love toward us by making open proclamation to the world that His dearest possession, His own Mother, was to be our Mother. "When Jesus, therefore, saw His Mother and the disciple John standing by whom He loved, then He said to His Mother, 'Woman, behold thy son,' and to the disciple he said, 'Behold thy Mother'" (Jn 14:26–27). One has only to read the Gospels and Epistles of Saint John to perceive, as we have seen, how he burned with the love of his divine Master dwelling in him. From that moment on, as a son to his mother, he took Mary to his heart. He was to relive the life of Jesus in his, as he watched over and cared for Jesus' Mother.

These words of Christ on the cross were not symbolical only, but effective! For just as He made Saint John the representative of the race of man for whom He suffered and died, so He made His Mother the Mother of all men by her becoming the Mother of the Beloved Disciple.

We her children are witnesses to the pangs of spiritual childbirth on Calvary, for as Jesus died for all men, the Mother who gave Him to us in turn was given to be our Mother, that she might watch over and care for our supernatural upbringing so that all of us might be made conformable to the image of Her Son and continue to relive His life through us.

The thought that my heavenly Mother is God's own masterpiece leaves me utterly bewildered. I know if I had the power to create my mother, I would have made her the most perfect of all creations. But the Son of God had that power! No wonder Saint Bonaventure cried out, "Though God could create a more perfect world, He could not create a more perfect mother than the Mother of God." And this Woman is *my* Mother! What a joy to know that I, therefore, having the most perfect Mother, will always be cared for and protected in a most perfect way from harm. If I start to swerve from the path, she will take me by the hand and lead me back to safety. My relationship to Mary reminds me of the story about the small boy who is crossing the street with his mother. With his hand firmly in hers, he isn't afraid of the dangers. He has complete confidence in his mother leading him to safety. Suddenly he trips, stumbles, and falls. Almost with reproach in his eye he looks up at his mother and cries, "Mommy, why don't you watch where I'm going?"

I, too, am crossing the dangerous road of life in order to reach the other side in safety, but I know with Mary, my Mother, by my side and with her hand in mine I have nothing to fear. If I stumble and fall, she will always be there to lift me up and lead me in safety to the other side. I, with the life of Jesus dwelling in me cannot fail, for Mary is my Mother!

God Bless and keep you in His Sacred Heart now and forever.

### God Is Everywhere

It was an awesome and impressive sight to see our three astronauts on television orbiting about the moon for the first time in the history of the world, but it was still more breathtaking to hear the Word of God coming back to earth when they quoted from the Book of Genesis in the Old Testament. "In the beginning God created heaven and earth..."

Truly, how small the earth then appeared to be! Thrown out on the immense sea of the universe, it seemed to be but a tiny pebble among the almost limitless galaxies of millions and millions of stars, all of which God holds in the palm of His hand! And yet, this same God chose our infinitesimally small world to become man and dwell among us! "Why?"—we ask, over and over again! And the only answer is that He loves man, His own image, with a passion equal only to the divine—a love that is infinitely beyond our finite minds to comprehend.

When we were asked the question as little children, "Where is God?," the answer came quickly to our lips. "God is everywhere." But how difficult such a simple answer is to comprehend! Has not each one of us wondered just what God in Himself is like—this all-powerful Being Who can be everywhere at one and the same time? I know I have! Many years ago, when we were being instructed on how to pray, we were told to place ourselves in the presence of God. But how could we do this? What was God like? Was He some kind of a tremendous Being, a sort of an ever-seeing, long-bearded, benevolent overseer with His arms outstretched over the whole world? Sometimes He is painted in such a manner, but such a picture is a pure figment of the imagination and has no reality whatsoever outside the mind. God in His essence is not human at all. He is divine in nature. But I have to admit that all my mental wrestling brought me little success in trying to imagine the infinite majesty and power of the Almighty upon Whom I depend for everything I have and everything I am. I was still unable to feel that real closeness to Him, or be aware of His presence in facing the ordinary, prosaic activities of everyday living.

But God Himself solved this problem by relating Himself to man in a visible, tangible, sensible way by becoming man—assuming a human nature exactly like ours with a human soul, mind, and will, like us in everything except sin. Now, it was so much easier to put myself in the presence of God through the Humanity of Jesus Christ, the Son of God. Now, no one could ever say, "God, up in the far-away heavens, or wherever You are, You don't know what crosses I have to carry, what sufferings I have to bear! You don't know what it is to be misunderstood and thought little of—to be a failure and laughed at! You don't know what it is to be a man!" No—for God does know, because He became one of us here in this world! So now to put ourselves in the presence of God is to contemplate our Savior, Jesus Christ, when He was here on earth; hear the words that fell from His blessed lips as He preached words of encouragement and understanding; watch Him as he moved about among the people bringing comfort, strength, and forgiveness to all who came to Him; even feel the warmth of His joyful presence as He repeats to each one of us, "Come to Me, all you who labor and are heavily burdened, and I will refresh you" (Mt 11:20).

Yes, here at last was a powerful way to acquire an awareness of the presence of God. But there was still another way of experiencing His presence, even in a more intimate, personal manner. This would be through His divine indwelling within our souls by the life of grace. By the very fact that He assumed a Human nature, He necessarily limited Himself to the narrow confines of Palestine, and the number of people whom He contacted was very limited. Then He died and left this world. Yet He was launching a program for salvation of souls that was to last until the end of time. How was He to accomplish this?

He would do it through other willing humanities. Each one of us would become His other-self in the era of time and the world in which we live. "I have come," He said, "that you may have life, and have it more abundantly" (Jn 10:10). "Abide in Me as I in the Father" (Jn 15:9). And through the life of grace which He merited for us by becoming man, we now have the presence of God—the Blessed Trinity Itself—within our very souls every second of our life here on earth, and this life of union with Him will be consummated in the Beatific Vision through the eons of eternity.

God Bless and keep you in His Sacred Heart now and forever.

*Man, an Extension of the Blessed Trinity*
Some years ago, I had the privilege of making a "Better World Retreat" under the direction of *Fr. Ricardo Lombardi, S.J.,* a renowned preacher and retreat master from Italy. I would like to pass on a few ideas to you.

God in Himself is a community: the three divine Persons in one divine nature. He willed to extend His community of three Persons to millions of persons like Himself. In His divine plan, He willed to create man after His own image, and communicate love, joy, and divine life. Through this divine communication, we become sons of God, our Heavenly Father. This first communication of divine life was lost by our First Parents, but "happy fault" it was, as Saint Augustine said: "by reason of this fault the Heavenly Father, moved by the Holy Spirit of divine love, sent His only begotten Son, Jesus Christ, to become man." By

His becoming man He would unify man, and all of us would become members of His Mystical Body, lifted up to the life of God Himself.

Jesus Christ is the Son of God by nature; we are the sons of God by adoption. By reason of this adoption, we can truly call God "Our Father," and know that He loves each one of us with the same infinite love that He loves His Eternal Son. Adopted children are loved as much as natural children and share equally in the inheritance with them. It follows, then, that we have our divine Savior to be our Brother and share equally with Him as co-heirs of the kingdom of Heaven.

A father's thought was in the mind of God, and a father's love in the heart of God when He created me personally. He gave me a share, not only in His Being, gave me not only life, but a share in His own divine life, so that I might not be just another creation, but His child—and that forever in the Blessed Trinity.

Everlasting union with the Blessed Trinity is my destination, not by the force of my own nature, but by the divine adoption of my Father in Heaven. No wonder Saint John could exclaim in wonderment, "Behold, what manner of love the Father has bestowed upon us that we should be called the children of God, and such we are" (1 Jn 3:1). Saint Paul, too, over and over again, speaks of our divine sonship, as he wrote to the Romans, "You have received a spirit of adoption as sons, by virtue of which we cry, Abba (Father). For the Spirit Himself gives testimony to our spirit that we are the sons of God" (Rom 8:15–16)! Saint Peter expressed it in these words, "We are partakers of His divine nature" (2 Pt 1:4). By this participation, of course, we are not God, but as His sons, we participate in His divine activity through the gift of sanctifying grace merited by the life and death of Jesus Christ, His Eternal Son. He takes up His life in us through this life of grace and bilocates Himself through our humanity. Not that we are in any way equal to God, but He, our loving Father, permits us to participate in His divine activity—His supernatural operations through the indwelling of His divine Son. Christ multiplies Himself through this divine indwelling over and over again. Each one of us relives every phase of His life here on earth—His joyful, His sorrowful, and we shall share in His glorious life—and that forever. This is the divine plan of God to extend His community of the Blessed Trinity; this is the consummation of perfect love; this is Heaven.

But we cannot reach this complete oneness with God in Heaven unless we are willing to go all the way with Jesus Christ here on earth. Saint Peter sets an example for us in this regard. Human as he was, and frightened at the prospect of dying for Christ during the early persecutions, he was hurrying out of Rome when he met Christ carrying His cross on the way into Rome. When Peter asked Christ where He was going, our divine Lord answered, "Back to Rome to be crucified again in your place." That was enough for Peter. He turned around and rushed back to Rome to be crucified right there in the Eternal City, just like his Master had been in Jerusalem—only upside down. We can almost hear him joyfully exclaiming to his executioners, "I am not worthy to die the way my Master did, but if you must crucify me, crucify me with my head downwards."

Today our divine Lord is speaking to each one of us as He did to Peter—to follow Him all the way in life and in death or whatever is asked of us, so that in the end we might share with Him the life and love of our Eternal Father and the Holy Spirit for all eternity.

God Bless and keep you in His Sacred Heart now and forever.

*Mirroring the Inner Vision*

As a young child I remember a particular picture in our home which impressed itself so deeply upon my mind that through all these ensuing years, I've never forgotten it. It was a painting of a beautiful woman sitting on top of the world, and at the bottom were penned the words, "The best of everything on earth is you, Jean dearest."

I'll not forget these words, for they were written by my father to my mother, and I know how they welled up from the very depths of his heart and soul and clamored for expression in words of love. I'm sure he recognized in her a reflection, as it were, of the beauty, goodness, sweetness, purity, and loveliness of God Himself, and every vibration of his heart went out to her in love. To him she truly was a mirror of the inner vision of the Creator in Whom is all perfection. I only hope and pray that someday I shall share their happiness, for they have both long since gone "home" to Him.

Isn't it true that love knocks at the gate of the soul and all but bursts the thin wall of the body as it cries out for some kind of external expression of the inner vision of God dwelling there? One might go so far as to say that there would not be a single masterpiece of painting, sculpture, or art in the world if there were not some deep-hidden, powerful love challenging the mind and heart of man to reproduce—as far as humanly possible in external achievement—some of the beauty and perfection of the divine Source of it all. For even though the daring efforts of the artist or the painter or the sculptor fall far short of this inner fire of divine artistry and perfection working within their souls, still a tiny spark of it breaks through to give us the great masterpieces in the world today.

Certainly anyone who has listened to this voice within his heart must be aware of the manner in which this divine love hurtles over space and time, defies separation and death itself, and announces its encouraging message of everlasting life. For when God chose to create man after His own image and likeness, it was almost as though He took a mirror and seeing a reflection of Himself, breathed into it the breath of life. In beholding man He cannot help but see Himself, and thus we might say, putting it in human language, every fiber of His infinite truth, goodness, and love goes into His masterpiece of creation.

How consoling it is to realize that because God's love is so great, there is in each of us this same spark of divine indwelling. His love is so intense that He was not content with giving us only natural human life, but a share in His own divine, supernatural life. Human by nature, yes, we are now divine by grace—the adopted children of God, the Father; co-heirs with Jesus Christ for the kingdom of Heaven; sacred temples of the Holy Spirit; living tabernacles of the Triune God Himself—all because God loves us so much. Now we can go about our everyday duties with the inner consciousness that we're never alone—that our divine Lord Himself uses our humanity to bless our little world wherever we may go or happen to be. Through us radiates the peace and joy of the vision of God's life to all with whom we come in contact.

And for ourselves an awareness of this great mystery gives us new enthusiasm and courage to be cheerful in the midst of trial and suffering, to be at peace in the throes of temptation and heartache, to keep strong on the royal road of the cross—for now we have the strength of divine life to sustain us.

The words of the beloved disciple, Saint John, "God is love and he who abides in love, abides in God and God in him," (1 Jn 4:16) are emphasized over and over again by Saint Paul and the Fathers of the Church. One most striking example of this is the admonition of Saint Paul to the Corinthians, "Do you not know that your body is a temple of the Holy Spirit within, whom you have from God, and that you are not your own? For you have been purchased at a price. Therefore, glorify God in your body" (1 Cor 6:19–20). Saint Augustine in the fourth century breathed the happy words, "This wonderful union which is properly called indwelling differs only in degree, or state, from that which beautifies the saints in Heaven." In all truth, we can say then that when our soul is in God's friendship in the state of grace, it is not only the vestibule of Heaven, but the living temple of the Blessed Trinity.

Truly, this is the secret of sanctity—herein lies the power of holiness, for by this divine life we become a mirror reflecting the inner vision of God Himself in a world that needs Him so much.

God Bless and keep you in His Sacred Heart now and forever.

*Explaining Our Faith*

In the world of rapid communications today, there is certainly a greater understanding regarding religious faiths among peoples of whatever race or creed everywhere, but even so there are still some false ideas concerning the Catholic Faith. To correct even one of such erroneous notions is of tremendous value. This was never so forcefully brought home to me as on the occasion when I asked a young man whom I had taught for a year if he ever thought of going ahead and learning more about the Catholic Faith. "Oh, I could never be a Catholic," he answered. "Why not?" I asked. His answer shocked me! "Because you Catholics believe that Mary is divine—that she is a goddess, and I could never accept that."

Suffice it to say that I explained in short order that such was not the truth at all, and that if a Catholic worshiped Mary as divine he would be guilty of serious sin. "She is a creature," I went on to explain, "and in no sense of the word is she, or can she, ever be on an equal plane with the Creator. She was created by God and remains on this finite level. Of course, of all God's creations she is His masterpiece because He chose her from all mankind to be His Mother, the channel through whom He would come to earth." I quickly added, "If you had the power of creating your own mother, wouldn't you have made her as perfect as possible? God had that power, and that's exactly what He did—but she is still not divine."

He breathed a sigh of relief with this hurried explanation, almost as though a great burden was lifted from his shoulders. Now he opened up his mind to a clearer explanation of other truths.

I have found this young man's case to be a rather ordinary one, for once the error is dispelled or clarified, the individual can hardly wait to learn more about religion and the basic truths that affect his daily living. It is truly amazing how much interest in the Faith can be generated by clearing up just one little problem. But I would say right here and now that these questions should not be left only to the priests to answer. Everyone should be prepared to answer the common objections and problems that arise, and if he is not so prepared to be humble enough to admit it, and then do a little bit of extra investigation and reading on the subject under discussion.

Strange as it may seem to us, we probably know a great deal more about our Faith than we give ourselves credit for. Of course, we must never forget that the grace of God is always there to be of help, and if we are sincere, our divine Lord Himself, [who] said, "Do not be concerned what you will say—it will be given to you," will work in and through us if we have confidence in Him. We must never give the impression that we are out to snare others, or rope them in, but when we ourselves are sincere in our belief and present a convincing example of living Christianity, others cannot help but be drawn to listen to our words and follow our example.

It seems to me that many non-Catholics are kept from the Church by misunderstanding, not the essential doctrines, but matters of secondary importance at best, such as statues, medals, pictures, candles, incense, and other practical means the Church institutes to foster devotion. Actually when the one seeking information about these matters is told that they are simply meant as aids to devotion and are reminders of the spiritual side of life, and that they do not contain any magical powers and are not really necessary at all, most of their difficulties are immediately solved. As far as the saints are concerned, why do we reverence them? It is the same idea as the honor we give to those who are dear to us, or our national heroes who have fought the good fight here on earth, and are now with God in Heaven. God honors His heroes, so why shouldn't we?

Now and then some people come up with the age-worn objections regarding the compatibility of divine revelation and science. This is easily answered by stating that the Author and Architect of both is the Omnipotent God, and there cannot possibly be a conflict or contradiction between them. If there appears to be such, it is definitely a lack of scientific research or a not having a proper and intelligent understanding of what God has revealed. We hold the Bible to be the revealed Word of God, but it must be interpreted in the light of the times during which it was written. It is certainly not a collection of mere pious myths or folklore. Catholics are encouraged to read the Bible daily in a spirit of prayer, learn from it, and be nourished by it.

Other questions also, such as on divorce and remarriage, the Church's stand on birth control and abortion, the Holy Eucharist and confession, and any other pertinent questions can be stated in reasonable plain terms exactly what we believe and hold, not with the idea of convincing the questioner then and there, but of aiding him to better understand our position. In this way we often find that all of us, no matter what Faith or belief we hold, are much closer than we ever imagined. "Good example" is the most eloquent sermon we can ever preach and will do far more towards uniting Christendom than the most persuasive arguments.

God Bless and keep you in His Sacred Heart now and forever.

*Love Calls for Union*
How true it is when we love someone very much we want to be near the one we love. Such is the love between a devoted husband and wife, or a loving child and his parent, or a young man engaged to the girl of his dreams.

So it is with the greatest man who ever walked this earth—really, greater than man because He was God—Jesus Christ. He came into this world with one burning desire—to be near those whom He loved—to unite Himself with each one of us in a bond so close and intimate that it is like the union between His Eternal Father and Himself. "Holy Father," He prayed for His apostles at the Last Supper, "keep in Thy Name those whom Thou hast given me, that they may be one even as we are . . . Yet not for those only do I pray, but for those also who through their word are to believe in Me, that all may be one, even as Thou, Father, in Me and I in Thee, that they may be one, even as we are one: I in them and Thou in Me" (Jn 17:11, 20–21).

Isn't this wonderful—the two of us are one—Jesus and I—by means of this divine life which He came into this world to share with man! "I have come that you may have life," He says, "and have it more abundantly" (Jn 10:10). "I am the way, the truth and the life" (Jn 14:6). What an exchange! Jesus Christ is the bridge between the infinite and the finite—linking humanity to divinity—and thus lifting men up to a participation in the supernatural life of God Himself.

This union between Christ and myself is so necessary in order to preserve this divine life dwelling in me that if I be separated from Him for one instant I will wither away and die. "I am the vine and you are the branches," He warns, "He who abides in Me, and I in him, he bears much fruit; for without Me you can do nothing (Jn 15:5). As the Father has loved Me, I also have loved you. Abide in My love" (Jn 15:9). No wonder each of us should pray from the depths of our soul, "Oh divine Savior, permit me never to be separated from Thee!"

Saint Paul was so overpowered by the necessity of keeping this living union between Christ and himself that he cried out, "I am sure that neither death, nor life, nor angels, nor principalities, nor things present, nor things to come, nor powers, nor height, nor depth, nor any other creature will be able to separate us from the love of God which is in Christ Jesus our Lord" (Rom 8:38–39). He spoke as though Christ Himself were speaking through him, "With Christ I am nailed to the cross. I live, now not I, but Christ lives in me" (Gal 2:19–20).

Later, he proved in action how convinced he was of the power and strength of Christ's divine life flowing through him. He was preaching to the early Christians in the town of Troas. Carried away by his burning zeal to spread the love of Christ among his listeners and to explain this living union between Christ and those who love him through sanctifying grace and the reception of Holy Communion, he forgot time and went on until midnight.

Saint Luke narrates in the Acts of the Apostles that "a certain young man named Eutychus, who was sitting on the window sill was sinking into a deep sleep as Paul talked on and on. Once overcome by sleep, he fell down from the third story and when he was picked up, he was dead. Paul went down, threw himself upon him, and said as he embraced him, 'Don't be alarmed; there is life in him'" (Acts 20:9–10). The great apostle, practicing what he preached, not in the least shaken by the incident, standing up in their midst and raising his hands over the people in silent prayer for a moment, must have reassured them that there was nothing to worry about, that he could do all things in Him Who strengthened him. The next moment that boy who had been dead got up alive, with vital blood coursing through his veins once again.

Who performed that stupendous miracle? Was it Paul? No, for no man has power over life and death! It was Jesus Christ Himself dwelling in him, using His ambassador as a willing instrument to prove that the lesson He was teaching, of His divine indwelling in those who love God and obey His Commandments, is true.

This brings to mind the little boy who was on his deathbed, and the priest asked him the question, "Son, are you afraid to die? "Afraid to die? No, I'm not afraid to die." "And why aren't you afraid?" the priest persisted. "Because I want to go where Jesus is." "But what if Jesus goes to Hell?" With a smile on his lips, the dying boy answered, "Where Jesus is, there is no Hell."

How true! What a consoling doctrine this is to know that we are never alone, that Christ is always with us no matter where we are or where we go; that in Him, we have the way, the truth and the life—and there is nothing that we two, working together as one, cannot accomplish here in time and for all eternity.

God Bless and keep you in His Sacred Heart now and forever.

## Special Love of Jesus for Little Children

As we study the life of our divine Master, we find that He had a special place in His Heart for little children. It was His delight to be in their midst—to romp and play with them and have them clamor around His knee as He told them stories in simple language of the love of God. He laid His hands upon them and on occasion embraced and blessed them. I like to imagine His curing the paralyzed, crippled bodies of His little ones, then picking them up on His shoulders, and running up and down along the shore of Lake Genesareth as He explains to them the beauty and majesty of God in every drop of water and grain of sand—or touching the eyes of little blind children and watching their expression of joy as wide-eyed, they look into His smiling face. How our divine Savior loved little children! When His apostles tried to shoo them away feeling they were annoying Him, He gently reprimanded them for their unwarranted concern. "Suffer the little children to come unto Me, and forbid them not, for of such is the kingdom of God" (Lk 18:16). How highly He valued their purity of soul and angelic innocence He proved when holding a child close to His Heart, He said to His disciples: "Amen, I say to you, unless you become converted and become as little children, you shall not enter the kingdom of Heaven. Whosoever therefore shall humble himself as this little child, he is the greater in the kingdom of Heaven. And he that shall receive one such child as this, receives Me" (Mt 18:3–5).

Never once did He ever scold a child, nor hesitate to take "time out" to be with them. And when they would come to Him with their little toys and playthings, He would be as interested in those as though the most important event of history was taking place.

Is it any wonder then that when our divine Lord instituted the sacrament of the Holy Eucharist that He was eager to have little children through all the ages of Christianity welcome Him often in Holy Communion! He yearns to be close to them today just as much as He did centuries ago when He was here on earth in His Humanity. No one knows better than He that those little ones of His would always be a source of consolation to His bleeding Heart when they would become one with Him through the Living Bread of His own Body and Blood in Holy Communion.

There lived a little boy some years ago who seemed to be very intimately aware of this close union between our Savior and himself, and even though he was only five years old, he had a burning desire to receive Him in Holy Communion. Frankie—that was his name—was the oldest of four children, and with his golden locks, looked just like a picture of the Christ Child. The little boy had a deep insight into the love of the Sacred Heart and had expressed his desire to be a priest from the age of two. His mother made him vestments with a golden chasuble like a priest wears at Mass, and of course he had a play altar. It was heartwarming to watch the little fellow as he pretended he was saying Mass. He would turn around with his arms wide and say: "*Dominus vobiscum*," (for Mass was said in Latin at that time) which means, "The Lord be with you," like a priest at the altar. One day while I was visiting the family, he delivered a sermon on the love of our divine Savior that fairly took my breath away. In his childlike expression, he compared God to Santa Claus. "You know," he said, "at Christmas time, Santy comes down the chimney and brings us all kinds of toys and things to make us happy, but Santy wouldn't have any toys at all to give away unless God first made the trees from which he could put the toys together." It was beautiful!

God must have loved Frankie very much, for He wanted him all for Himself—to be right in His Sacred Heart—as His little tabernacle. The child was suddenly stricken with a very serious disease and within a few days was lying next to death's door in the hospital. They had him in an oxygen tent, and for a while he was able to pretend he was a soldier fighting for his King. He clenched a small crucifix in his tiny fist until he was too weak to hold it any longer—then a nurse pinned it to his pillow and he was satisfied. When she asked him what he wanted to be when he grew up, he answered, "I want to be a priest!" "Why?" the nurse asked. "Because I want to hold the Baby Jesus up as a priest does at Mass—because I love the Baby Jesus."

Frankie's Baby Jesus must have loved him very much, because He came all the way down from Heaven—the child made his First Holy Communion on his deathbed—and then the Lord of Heaven and earth held His little Frankie by the hand and took him up to Heaven. Frankie died—yes—but he died in the embrace of the one Whom he loved above all else—our divine Jesus, Who has time and time again manifested His special love for little children. This little boy desired to receive Holy Communion so ardently that our loving Savior could not resist his prayer. A little angel left this materialistic world to fly into the very Heart of Jesus to be with Him for all eternity.

All of us can derive a lesson from this, for if we become as little children—small in our own eyes, but big in the eyes of God, we too will radiate His love and have a special place in His Sacred Heart—now and always.

God bless and keep you in His Sacred Heart now and forever.

# 6

# Biographical Data of Cora Louise Evans

*Diocese of Salt Lake City, Utah*

| | |
|---|---|
| *July 9, 1904* | Birth, Midvale, Utah; child of Laura and Robert Yorgason |
| *1912* | Cora is baptized a Mormon (8 years old) |
| *June 4, 1924* | Mormon Marriage to Mack Evans, Mormon temple in Salt Lake City (this location is the worldwide headquarters for the Mormon Church). |
| | Cora completely rejects Mormon religion based on the secret ritual and what she considers to be false teachings about God. Cora begins ten-year search for the true religion. |
| *Dec. 9, 1934* | Future Catholic bishop is catalyst for Cora's conversion—Ogden, Utah: Cora listens to radio talk by Monsignor Duane Hunt (later he would become Most Reverend Hunt, Bishop of Salt Lake City), decides to visit local Catholic Church. |
| *Mar. 30, 1935* | Cora baptized a Catholic by Father William E. Vaughn, Saint Joseph Catholic Church, Ogden, Utah. |
| *Mar. 31, 1935* | Cora receives her First Holy Communion. |

| | |
|---|---|
| *1936–1939* | Influences Mormon conversions—Cora influences more than 1000 Mormons to visit Saint Joseph Catholic Church, numerous conversions follow. |
| *July 1938* | Ogden, Utah: mysticism—During this deep ecstasy Cora makes choice to serve God for the rest of her life. Describes state of her soul as being intimately united to God. Cora refers to this as her "vow day." |

## Archdiocese of Los Angeles, California

| | |
|---|---|
| *Mar. 17, 1941* | Cora moves to Southern California and is active at Saint Cecilia's Parish. |
| *May 21, 1942* | Apparition of Saint Aloysius Gonzaga |
| *Feb. 20, 1945* | Father Frank Parrish, S.J. (1911–2003) appointed confessor and spiritual director by Father Joseph King, S.J., Provincial of the California Province of the Society of Jesus |
| *Dec. 24, 1946* | Mission entrusted to Cora Evans revealed to her by Jesus. Cora learns she is to promulgate the Mystical Humanity of Christ (the divine indwelling) within souls—as a way of prayer in the United States and throughout the world. Jesus promises to foster the devotion. |
| *1945–1957* | Based on ecstasies, and in complete obedience to her spiritual director, Cora writes numerous profound manuscripts and diaries.<br>Mystical phenomena witnessed by priests, religious, and lay people. Many testimonies are written. |
| *July 30, 1947* | Stigmata—Cora begins experiencing the stigmata. She endures frequent pain for the rest of her life in the palms of her hands, head (crown of thorns), feet, and over her heart. |

| | |
|---|---|
| *1948* | Cora prays that our Lord will allow her to be like the Little Flower, Saint Thérèse, helping souls on earth after her death. |

## *Diocese of Monterey, California*

| | |
|---|---|
| *1956* | Cora moves to Boulder Creek in Northern California, Saint Michael Parish. |
| *Jan. 4, 1957* | Most Reverend Duane Hunt (1884–1960), Bishop of the Diocese of Salt Lake City, visits Cora at her home in Boulder Creek, California. |
| *Mar. 30, 1957* | Cora enters Eternal Life. Twenty-two years earlier on this same date, March 30 (1935), Cora was baptized a Catholic. Burial in crypt in the Fatima Wing of the mausoleum adjacent to the site where the California Jesuits are buried in Santa Clara, California. |
| *1992* | Michael McDevitt appointed custodian for the writings and promoter of the Mystical Humanity of Christ, the mission entrusted to Cora Evans by our Lord |
| *Dec. 29, 2003* | Father Frank Parrish, S.J. enters eternal life. |
| *June 15, 2010* | Cause for Cora Evans opened and announced by Most Reverend Richard Garcia, D.D., Bishop of Monterey, California. |
| *Feb. 18, 2011* | Imprimatur granted for prayer for the intercession of Servant of God Cora Evans by Most Reverend George Niederauer, D.D., Archbishop of San Francisco. |
| *Oct. 2014* | *The Refugee from Heaven* by Cora Evans published; available on CoraEvans.com. |

*Importance of this cause for the Church*

The cause for *Cora Evans* is for the good of the whole Church. She is an ideal model of a married woman, a mother, and a convert who influenced many conversions to Catholicism. As a convert from Mormonism she suffered humiliation and the loss of friends and family. Many parents will identify with Cora as a mother who suffered the loss of a child. Throughout her life she experience physical suffering. This included the pain of the stigmata, which she endured for her faith.

Cora Evans was obedient to her spiritual director in all matters concerning the guidance of her soul, and she was committed to the teaching authority of the Catholic Church. Cora searched for the truth and was a person for whom Jesus was a constant companion in the ordinary circumstances of her life, and in a unique way as a mystic. Her many heroic virtues define Cora as a person who presents the faithful with a good example of persistence, courage, faith, and charity.

The story of Cora's life and the heroic choices she made, the untold personal sacrifices and suffering she endured for the cause of our Catholic faith, her writings, and her outstanding evangelical virtues qualify her as a person worthy of emulation.

*The Cause for Cora Evans benefits the Universal Church*

Our Lord entrusted her with the promulgation of the *Mystical Humanity of Christ* as a way of prayer for the faithful throughout the United States and eventually the world. This way of prayer, living with a heightened awareness of the living, indwelling presence of Jesus, is reaching into the daily lives of people and spreading its roots in the western United States and beyond. It is Eucharistic spirituality—so important for the growth of the Church in our country. In recent times over 10,000 members of the faithful have attended parish retreats, and major events have been held for the entire Archdiocese of San Francisco and the Diocese of Salt Lake City. Popular piety is growing at a steady pace nationwide.

7

# Prayer for the Intercession of Cora Evans

Composed by *Father Frank Parrish, S.J.* (1911–2003)

*First—Visit the Blessed Sacrament*
CORA PRAYED that she would be given the same gift as Saint Thérèse, the Little Flower, spending her heaven on earth doing good. Cora promised to pray for all who asked for her intercession, "I will answer every prayer providing it is first preceded by a visit to the Most Blessed Sacrament."

*Second—The Prayer—Ask Cora to intercede in your behalf*
Dearest Jesus, You blessed Cora Evans with many supernatural mystical gifts as a means of drawing us to a deeper and more intimate union with your Sacred Heart through Your divine indwelling, Your Mystical Humanity. I ask You, through her intercession, to help me in my special request (name the favor) and my efforts to do Your will here on earth and be with You, Your Blessed Mother, Saint Joseph, and the whole court of Heaven forever.

*Third— Say three times*
Our Father, Hail Mary, Glory Be to the Father

IMPRIMATUR Granted
Most Reverend George H. Niederauer, DD, Ph.D.
*Archbishop of San Francisco,* February 18, 2011

The faithful are encouraged to acknowledge favors received. See contact information on the back cover.

*Daily Spiritual Communion*
*"Lord, I empty myself of self and invite you to relive Your Mystical Humanity, Your resurrected life, through me today."* With this prayer you commit to taking HIM with you wherever you go.

"May God bless you with all the desires of the Eternal Father and bless the wishes of your soul."